AUG 21 2008

Speed Training For

M000006135

DISCARDED

Produced in English with the financial assistance of the ITF

MANFRED GROSSER
HEINZ KRAFT
RICHARD SCHÖNBORN

SPEED TRAINING FOR

TENNIS

Braselton Library
Braselton, Georgia
DISCARDED

MEYER & MEYER SPORT

Original title: Schnelligkeitstraining im Tennis
– Sindelfingen: Sportverlag Schmidt&Dreisilker GmbH, 1998
Translated by Heather Ross

British Library Cataloguing in Publication Data
A catalogue record for this book is available from the British Library

Grosser/Kraft/Schönborn:
Speedtraining for Tennis / Manfred Grosser; Heinz Kraft; Richard Schönborn.
[Transl.: Heather Ross]
– Oxford : Meyer und Meyer Sport (UK) Ltd., 2000
ISBN 1-84126-030-4

All rights reserved. Except for use in a review, no part of this publication may be
reproduced, stored in a retrieval system, or transmitted, in any form or by any
means now known or hereafter invented without the prior written permission of
the publisher. This book may not be lent, resold, hired out or otherwise disposed
of by way of trade in any form, binding or cover other than that which is
published, without the prior written consent of the publisher.

© 2000 by Meyer & Meyer Sport (UK) Ltd.
Oxford, Aachen, Olten (CH), Vienna,
Québec, Lansing/ Michigan, Adelaide, Auckland, Johannesburg, Budapest
Member of the world
Sportpublishers' Association (WSA)
Photos : Sportverlag Schmidt&Dreisilker GmbH, Sindelfingen
Cover photo: Bongarts Sportfotografie GmbH, Hamburg
Cover design: Birgit Engelen, Stolberg
Editorial: John Coghlan, Winfried Vonstein
Cover and type exposure: frw, Reiner Wahlen, Aachen
Printed in Germany
by Druckpunkt Offset GmbH
ISBN 1-84126-030-4
e-mail: verlag@meyer-meyer-sports.com

Contents

Editors' Foreword 7
Authors' Foreword...........9

1   **Introduction:**
    10 points on the importance of speed in tennis...........10

2   **Some necessary theory** 11
2.1   What is speed?...........11
2.2   Some biologically and developmentally conditioned
    aspects and their significance in the game of tennis 15

3   **Overview of biological and practical**
    training goals and long-term planning...........21
3.1   What are training goals?...........21
3.2   What is long-term planning? 22

4   **Training methods and exercises**...........23
4.1   General methodical hints 23
4.2   "Learning" and training of time-programmes 24
4.2.1   Definition and methodical hints 24
4.2.2   Exercises to form time-programmes by jumps...........26
4.2.3   Exercises to form time-programmes by throws...........28
4.2.4   Exercises to form time-programmes by services...........29
4.3   Training of reaction speed and action velocity...........30
4.3.1   Definition and methodical hints 30
4.3.2   Exercises to improve reaction speed
    and action velocity without anticipation...........32
4.3.3   Exercises to improve reaction speed
    and action velocity with anticipation 43
4.4   Training of frequency speed...........47
4.4.1   Definition and methodical hints 47
4.4.2   Exercises to improve frequency speed with focus on legs...........49
4.4.3   Exercises to improve frequency speed
    with focus on shoulders/arms...........58

CONTENTS

4.5	Combined training of action velocity, frequency speed, strength-speed and coordinative abilities	61
4.5.1	Definition and methodical hints	61
4.5.2	Exercises for the combined improvement of action velocity, frequency speed, strength-speed and coordinative abilities	62
4.6	Training of complementary performance-determining factors	77
4.6.1	General comments	77
4.6.2	Strength training	77
4.6.2.1	Definition and methodical hints	77
4.6.2.2	Basic exercises to stabilise the abdomen and back muscles	80
4.6.2.3	Exercises to improve chest, shoulder and arm muscles by the basic method	84
4.6.2.4	Exercises to improve the hip and leg muscles by the basic method	91
4.6.2.5	Exercises to improve the hip and leg muscles by the speed-oriented maximum strength method	94
4.6.2.6	Explosive strength exercises to improve hip and leg muscles	96
4.6.2.7	Reactive strength exercises to improve foot, leg and hip muscles	97
4.6.2.8	Explosive strength exercises to improve shoulder and arm muscles	101
4.6.2.9	Reactive strength exercises to improve shoulder and arm muscles	105
4.6.2.10	Exercises to improve foot and leg muscles	107
4.6.3	Endurance training	114
4.6.3.1	Definition and methodical hints	114
4.6.3.2	Training programmes	116
4.6.4	Flexibility training	117
4.6.4.1	Definition and methodical hints	117
4.6.4.2	Exercises to improve flexibility	118
5	**Training programmes for short and medium term planning**	**129**
5.1	Training programmes for training units	129
5.1.1	Suggestions for the planning of training units	131
5.2	Training programmes for microcycles	134
	Bibliography and Authors' Profile	**135**

EDITOR'S
FOREWORD

The DTB/German Tennis Federation -Training Library aims to provide concrete advice for the variety of tennis coaching and training practices. This volume is intended to supplement the first ("Technique and Tactics") and second ("Teaching and Training") volumes, particularly in regard to their emphasis on practical tennis.

The DTB/German Tennis Federation -Training Library is intended primarily for all tennis coaches and instructors, because of its predominant orientation towards practical tennis. However, we also want to reach the players themselves, from beginner through developing to advanced players, so that they can improve their own game and, eventually, be able to get more pleasure for themselves, and if teachers for their pupils, from the game.

In conjunction with tennis technique, speed, especially the acceleration ability and the movement speed, is both a characteristic and match-deciding feature of the game of tennis. Despite this importance, speed has been inadequately dealt with in the tennis literature. A systematic introduction to the improvement of speed in practical tennis training has especially been lacking. This volume will finally fill this gap, particularly as the authors can prove decades sf succesful practical work in speed training with tennis players.

In accordance with the aim and the desired function of our DTB/German Tennis Federation -Training Library, the theoretical basics are set out as concisely and simply as possible, to leave enough room for practical aspects. This includes a detailed description of a variety of exercises especially intended for grooving performance for runs and throws, with the emphasis on reaction and action speed, and frequency speed intended for the improvement in isolation or in combination of relevant tennis-specific abilities. For the important connection between speed and other conditioning factors like strength , endurance and agility, other exercises are described in detail.

Specific information for the structuring of speed training within a training unit, or a weekly training plan, constitute the final part of the extensive practical section (a total of 155 exercises).

We, and the authors, hope for a wide readership and acceptance of this Volume by the DTB Training Library; and that it will be both useful and fun for all learning players.

Prof. Dr. Karl Weber
- DTB/German Tennis Federation Vice President -

Rüdiger Borneman
- Chief of the DTB Teaching Commitee -

FAUTHORS' OREWORD

Although speed is, along with technique and coordination, one of the most important performance-limiting factors in tennis, apart from a few exceptions it is mentioned seldom, if at all, in the specialist tennis literature. In the rare cases when hints for practical training are given, they are usually too short or too general and unsystematic.

When one considers that in championship tennis, according to court surface, a quarter to a third of all strokes are hit under time pressure (that is at least one stroke per point), then the influence of the various forms of speed on the match result is obvious.

The authors of this book have been very active in this and other special areas for decades, and set out the whole problem of speed in a systematic and tennis-specific way. They are convinced that this book will provide sufficient suggestions for optimal tennis-specific speed-training for a wide range of tennis coaches and active players.

Dr. Dr. h.c. Manfred Grosser
University Professor
Richard Schönborn
A-Coach German Tennis Federation

Heinz Kraft
Qualified Sports Teacher

INTRODUCTION

10 POINTS ON THE
IMPORTANCE OF SPEED IN TENNIS

1

The subject of this book will initially be presented by of the following 10 points:

- Speed or speed of movement is, along with coordination ability and feeling for movement, the decisive feature of many tennis-specific movements. In detail, one must:
- be able to react as fast as possible to surprise actions by an opponent;
- be able to move one's own body and the racquet as fast as possible in different directions;
- be able to burst of speed as fast as possible and sprint short distances, stop and start running again;
- be able to give the ball as much release velocity as possible in many strokes (e.g. in the service and the smash).
- and finally, combining speed with technical-tactical and conditioning abilities, be able to play the whole match as fast and as effectively as possible
- speed, as an isolated "pure" ability, does not exist in tennis; it is always just one factor of the complex movement or playing actions.
- an excellent technique level and well-defined coordination abilities allow speed to come into its own. Seen in this way, speed, co-ordination ability and technique are a "unit" in tennis.
- speed strength, basic endurance and optimal muscular stretchability have a positive effect on speed.
- muscular imbalance and lack of will-power lead to a considerable lack of speed- specific performance ability.

2 SOME NECESSARY THEORY

2.1 WHAT IS SPEED?

Speed in sport means the ability to achieve the highest possible reaction speed and movement speeds under certain given conditions, by means of the cognitive processes, maximal will-power and the functionality of the neuro-muscular system.

These "certain given conditions" include:
1. Beginning movements after a signal (=reaction time or *reaction speed* in tennis mainly on visual stimuli).
2. Separate movements (=speed in acyclic movements, also called *action velocity*; e.g. a tennis stroke, fast arm or leg movements).
3. Continuous regular movements (=speed in cyclic movements, also called *frequency speed*, e.g. short sprints, tapping).
4. Movement combinations or complex movements = in acyclic and cyclic movements, consecutive or combined, e.g. all fast match play actions; in most cases *fast strength* is conducive to speed.

In terms of physics, *speed* is measured as velocity and expressed as distance over time. For the diagnosis of special speed abilities we refer you to the relevant literature (Grosser/Starischka 1986; Grosser 1991; Martin et al. 1991; Lehmann 1993; Schmalz/T‚rk-Noack 1993; Voss/ Werthner 1994).

In the latest literature (compare Grosser 1991; Bauersfeld/Voss 1992; Lehmann 1993, Weigelt 1995; Grosser/Starischka 1998) a difference is made between "pure" and "elementary" *speed abilities* on the one hand, and "complex" ones on the other hand. This difference is based as much on empirical experience in practical sport as on the latest scientific knowledge.

Reaction speed is a special form of speed ability.

In Table 1 the various speed abilities (types of speed) and their primary influence components are presented according to the above theories.

Explanations

Reaction Speed

The *reaction* of a person is the behavioural response to a stimulus. Stimuli can also be called signals, which in sport can be acoustic (sound of the stroke), visual e.g. the moving ball, or tactile e.g. touch. We react fastest to the latter, and acoustic signals are "processed" somewhat faster than visual ones.

Reaction speed in sport is consequently the physical manifestation of reaction time, and is the time between the sending of a signal to a solicited muscle and the contraction or movement e.g. pressure with the feet onto the floor, before starting to the backswing. Reaction speed means the ability, to react as fast as possible to a stimulus.

Table 1: Types of speed and their primary influence components

Higher characterisation	Independent speed ability	Elementary speed abilities		Complex Speed Abilities			
Type of speed	reaction speed	action velocity	frequency speed	strength speed	sprinting strength	strength speed endurance	sprint endurance
Form of movement		acyclic	cyclic	acyclic	cyclic	acyclic	cyclic
Example	All game sports	(table) tennis stroke	fast foot drill, sprints	stroke, jump	running acceleration, kicks	fencing, boxing	sprints longer than 60m
Primary components of influence	anticipation, perception, information processing, Impulse transfer, Latency period	- time-programme, - inter muscular coordination		- time-programme, - speed-strénght		- time-programme, - specific endurance	

In tennis, pure reaction speed is particularly important, especially in the return of the first service, to reach a passing shot at the net or in a volleying duel in doubles. In practice though it is always connected to action velocity, and possibly required speed strength (explosive strength). Furthermore a successful action depends very strongly on excellent perception and anticipation abilities, for a pure motor reaction alone is not sufficient at extremely high ball speeds (approx. 0.4-0.7 sec.).

Elementary Speed Abilities

This means those speed abilities that are defined as elementary time-programmes (acyclic and cyclic type according to Bauersfeld/Voss 1992), therefore primarily depend on the quality of neuro-muscular control and regulatory processes (cf. also page 16). According to BAUERSFELD/VOSS (1992) and LEHMANN (1993), elementary time-programmes are not dependent on strength and sex. The term "time-programme" is, for these authors, synonymous with elementary speed, where the acyclic and cyclic forms are independent of each other. Elementary speed can simply be determined by a measurement of support time of a fastest possible drop jump from a height of 20-40cm, the cyclical speed by maximal speed foot tapping in a sitting position. In both measurements, a "speed quotient" for potential talent can be calculated. A high speed level means support times below 170 ms and frequencies above 12Hz/s (corresponding to short time-programmes). These elementary speed abilities are produced in movements with little or no external resistance. They can be divided into:

- *action velocity,* or the ability to carry out acyclic movements at the highest possible speed against low resistance e.g. leg lifting, (table) tennis strokes.

This ability is one of the performance-limiting factors in tennis and cannot be compensated for by any other factor. Its high quality is particularly indispensable in modern tennis, for all fast strokes must be perfectly finely-motor coordinated if they are to be carried out successfully. The basis of excellent action velocity is a high coordination ability (=interaction of central nervous system and the skeletal system) and coordination speed.

- *Frequency speed*, or the ability to carry out cyclic movements at high speeds against low resistance (e.g. fast foot drill, tapping, sprints).

In modern tennis this ability is also of great importance, in combination with other speed types, and cannot be compensated for. For example after correctly anticipating, reacting and starting in time, the distance to the hitting point (up to 14m) must be covered as fast as possible. Frequency speed is absolutely essential for this.

Complex Speed Abilities

These are complex forms of fast movement execution, which are influenced just as much by *strength and endurance abilities* and certain conditions as by the elementary speed abilities (control and regulatory processes). The "certain conditions" in tennis deal mainly with:

- the type of movement required like push-offs, turning, etc.
- the movement technique
- the size and duration of the resistance to be overcome (especially that of one's own body);
- individual precondition e.g. sex, development, constitutional characteristics;
- external and internal influences e.g. wind, opponent, spectators, condition of the court, psychological pressure, etc.

The complex speed abilities are used in movements against high external resistances (in tennis, especially one's own body weight) and in movements with a fatigue-conditioned performance decrease in long matches. They can be divided into:

- *strength speed:* the ability to carry out acyclic movements at high speeds against high resistance e.g. push off, takeoff for smash. It is synonymous with speed- or fast strength.

This ability alone is not performance-limiting, but it is of great importance as a precondition for the execution of any further action in tennis.

- *strength speed endurance*: the ability to carry out acyclic movements at high speeds in spite of fatigue-conditioned loss of speed e.g. frequent consecutive strokes or fast strokes in the 3rd to 5th set.

Signs of fatigue either in the leg or arm muscles, especially in long matches, is frequently the deciding reason for a performance breakdown in the fine motor system. The consequences are slower starts, weaker arm action, and in particular decreasing accuracy and the accumulation of miss-hits.

- *sprinting strength*: the ability to carry out cyclic movements at high speeds against external high resistance e.g. acceleration ability in short push-offs.

This ability is enormously important, especially for covering short distances under time pressure, e.g. after an opponent's well-placed volley or smash, in running for a drop shot, etc. It is not just a question of getting to the ball, but of reaching it in time to be able to hit an attacking shot.

- *sprint endurance*: the ability to resist a loss of speed caused by fatigue in maximal speed performances in cyclical movements.

SOME BIOLOGICAL AND
2.2 DEVELOPMENT-CONDITIONED ASPECTS

Biological bases for speed and knowledge of motor development processes in children and young people appear to many coaches as "superfluous theory". However, such knowledge gives coaches a better understanding of:

- the motor speed processes;
- the correct choice of training contents and methods in the different age groups;
- the connection with tennis-specific technique and technique training, and
- the short, middle and long-term planning of the total tennis performance.

Initially, in Table 2 there is a clear presentation of important human *biological* and some mental *"partial systems"*, and corresponding essential selected factors. A few of them are explained here in brief (for more detail see Grosser 1991).

Table 2: *Necessary adaptations in "Partial systems" for the patterning of motor speed.*

Neuromuscular System	Psychic System	Tendo-muscular System
• neuronal control and regulatory processes∕ time-programmes • stimulus channelling speed • pre-enervation • reflex enervation • inter-muscular coordination • intra-muscular coordination (recruiting, frequencing, synchronisation)	• concentration • perception • motivation • will power	• sectional area of fast-twitch fibres • stiffness • viscosity • energy supply (morphological, metabolism-conditioned)

By means of correct speed training, in connection with strength increase, these factors can, to an extent, be positively affected.

Neuronal Control and Regulatory Processes - Time-programmes

Elementary (pure) speed abilities are determined by the quality of neuro-muscular control and regulatory processes. They

1. are stored as elementary movement programmes (= time-programmes);
2. are connected by the patterning of nerve conduction speed, muscle-self reflex and muscle fibre structure (=all are genetically conditioned), and
3. go unconsciously, since the "running time" is less than 200ms (for further explanations cf. Grosser∕Starischka 1998).

Pre-enervation

is the activation of a muscle about 70-150 ms before the actual strength demand. It is a preliminary increase in tension in the contractile fibres and the fine recruiting of the muscle spindles. It is consequently part of a central nervous system movement programme and can be improved by speed training.

Reflex Enervation

is the activation of the muscles through the stretch reflex, which is triggered by the muscle spindle when a muscle is stretched (peak activity about 25-40 ms after start of stretch; it also appears in the stretch-shortening cycle; (for details see "Stiffness").

Inter muscular coordination

is the interaction of synergetically and antagonistically working muscles. This happens under centrally-programmed control (enervation of the muscles influenced by the cerebrum and cerebellum), and reflex control mechanisms consisting of the stretch reflex, reciprocally antagonistic inhibition, auto-inhibiting, reciprocally antagonistic stimulation and gamma enervation; (for details c.f. Grosser/Starischka 1998).

Intra-muscular coordination

is the synchronous activation (=synchronisation) of the motor units within a muscle. Effective here are:
1. Frequenting: graduation (regulation) of the stimulation (impulse/ second) from the motor cortex, and
2. Recruiting: assembling of a certain number of motor units.

The recruiting sequence is:
1. in all shows of strength: firstly the slow motor units (slow twitch fibres), then the weaker fast twitch fibres (FTO) then the stronger fast twitch fibres with large motor neurones and high exciting threshold;
2. in explosive strength tension: at 25% of maximal strength, simultaneous recruiting of all fibres (=synchronisation). In fast movements against low resistance it is mainly the fast twitch fibres (40-90 ms; slow twitch fibres 90-140 ms) that work;
3. in movements against high loads, and in slow strength tension, at 85-90% of maximal strength, all fibres are activated (further increase only possible by frequenting).
(Detailed explanations c.f. Tidow/Wiemann 1993).

Fibre type composition

We distinguish roughly between FTG, FTO and slow twitch fibres. The proportion of the sectional surface of fast twitch and slow twitch fibres is decisive. The fast twitch fibres have a higher contraction speed and double the tension development (=speed muscles).

For fibre alteration through training the following should be noted:

1. Fibre type alteration is very complex and not yet fully understood;
2. It is possible to change fast twitch fibres (IIb) by endurance training; fast twitch fibres can disappear completely. The alteration in slow fibres is a combination of functional adaptation and morphological transformation (Hoppeler 1992);
3. A fibre type change can also take place by strength training; according to STARON et al. (1991) and ADAMS et al. (1993), after 7 weeks of sectional training, a considerable reduction of the FTG-fibres occurs in favour of the FTO and slow twitch fibres, and after 13-20 weeks of hypertrophy training no IIb fibres whatever were detectable. With specific speed strength training it is possible to reverse this development (c.f. Tidow 1998);
4. A training-conditioned morphological change of slow twitch fibres into FTG fibres has not yet been demonstrated. By relevant selective strength training, however, the "whole" muscle can be made faster.

Physiological Muscle Cross Section

There exists a close connection between maximal strength and muscle cross-section. The strength values per cross-section area are: men $7kp/cm^2$; women: $6kp/cm^2$ (variation range: 3-12 Kp/cm^2). It is the physiological, not the anatomical, cross section which is decisive.

Stiffness (=Reactiv-power)

is the hardness of the muscle-tendon-tissue. It is of great importance in the so-called stretch-shortening cycle, which occurs in all drop jumps, and in games with short stops and subsequent immediate starts, and in the backwards and forwards movements of the arms and the trunk. It happens as follows:

1. short eccentric stretching of the muscules. Here the autonomous enervation and elasticity characteristics appear,
2. the concentric phase in which pre-activation, stored elastic tension energy and reflexivity flow to.

Table 3: Energy Supply in Fast Muscle Performance

Energy Store	Maximal Duration of work	Re synthesis
- ATP, Creatine P - anaerobic-alactic - highest flow rate	- up to 10 s (extreme: ~ 20) training effect: - ATP~ +50% - CrP~ +70%	Half value: ~ 15 s 90%: ~ 60 s 100%: ~ 2-3 min.
- glycogen - anaerobic-lactic	- up to 90 s - favourable, large store	Half life period (lactate): -at 5 mmol: ~10' -at 10 mmol: ~ 15' - at 20 mmol: ~ 25' 1-3h 100% regeneration

Muscle fibre cross section and composition, elasticity and enervation characteristics of muscles, tendons and ligaments (=reactive tension ability) are performance-determining. Stiffness is thus trainable.

Energy Production
(c.f. Table 3)
A further theoretical view is essential to in *Age Levels of Children and Young People* in connection with biological facts, and the parallel appearance of speed abilities. Since this area is extremely extensive we present the essential aspects only in the form of a table (c.f. Table 4; for more details see e.g. Asmus 1991; Martin et al. 1991; Charitinova 1993; Baur et al. 1994; Weineck 1994; Grosser/Starischka 1998). From this point of view it is important that optimal development of specific speed abilities depends on fixed age phases. We consider this again in connection with the order of training goals (c.f. Table 5).

Table 4: Motor Development Stages, Speed abilities and Training.

Age Group	Biological Facts	Sensitive Phases and Training	Performance complement abilities
6/7-9/10	• brain growth 95% • start of good movement coordination	(reaction speed) general reaction training	general coordination abilities
9/10-12/13	• brain maturity finished • very good movement coordination	• Time-programmes • reaction speed • frequency speed • action velocity	• special coordination abilities • complex muscle training
12/13-15/16	• slight coordination reduction • favourable strength speed	• Time-programmes • action velocity • strength speed	• dynamic and reactive speed strength • complex muscle training • aerobic capacity
from 15/16/17	• renewed good coordination	all speed abilities	• speed-oriented maximum strength • aerobic and anaerobic capacity

3 OVERVIEW OF BIOLOGICAL AND PRACTICAL TRAINING GOALS AND LONG TERM PLANNING

3.1   WHAT ARE TRAINING GOALS?

By *training goals* we mean defined performances, which are to be achieved in a certain period of time. In tennis, for example, reaching a higher playing level or the improvement in (world-) ranking lists are so-called *higher goals*, while the improvement of speed abilities is a so-called *specific goal*.

In long-term planning of later goals, along with practical goal setting, it is important for the coach to know the relevant biological goal aspects, and to consider the structure and preconditions of the type of sport. Also knowledge of the motor development processes e.g. age, growth, constitution, current performance condition etc. must be known. Only on this basis the correct choice of training contents and methods and optimal progress finally can be ensured.

In table 5 we present the biological and practical training goals for speed abilities. These training goals are in addition shown in table 4 in connection with the motor development stages, and the corresponding so-called sensitive phases between the ages of 6 and about 20. Both tables indicate so-called long-term performance planning.

Table 5: Training goals to improve speed abilities

Biological Training Goals	Practical Training Goals	Best age for optimal improvement
1. Training of neuro-muscular control and regulatory processes	1. "Learning" of time-programmes	From about 7 - 13/15
2. Improvement of intermuscular coordination in connection with control and regulatory mechanisms	2. Training of reaction, action velocity and frequency speed (technique!)	From about 9 - 15/16
3. Development of morphological structures and functional-energetic processes conditioning components.	3. Complementing of pure speed abilities (1. + 2.) with further performance determining elements	From about 12/15 to maturity

3.2   WHAT IS LONG-TERM PLANNING?

By *planning* we mean the direct practical influencing between coach and athlete/player, whereby the coach, due to his theoretical knowledge and his practical experience, tries to best coordinate all influencing aspects on performance development. Long-term performance planning from beginner to world-class level lasts about 10-15 years!

The whole speed area must be considered as one of the most important performance influencing factors of long-term planning.

As we have already shown in tables 4 and 5, in the separate age-groups there are different emphases which must be systematically developed according to biological age. Omissions in this development can not be made up for later. A potential top player can be prevented from, or hindered in reaching elite level at an early age already.

Every coach is therefore well-advised, during the course of the separate development phases of childhood, to emphasise at least the same attention to speed as he does to technique development or coordination training.

4 TRAINING METHODS AND EXERCISES

4.1 GENERAL METHODICAL HINTS

Below is a presentation of selected tried and tested (by the authors and other experts) examples of training exercises (=training contents) and training methods to improve tennis players' speed abilities.

The separate speed abilities are each defined briefly again in the beginning and set out with important methodical hints for practical application.

The following *general methodical guidelines* are basically valid for speed training:

- In speed training, quality comes before quantity, i.e. fastest possible speed is created by a highly marked complex control and regulatory process between the brain and muscles. Speed must be both, trained and learnt.
- Speed in sport is only "learnable" and "trainable" by special exercises, not general ones. These special exercises must partially or completely consist of the temporal-spatial, dynamic and energetic features of the competition movements. These are the resulting consequences for
  - *Basic Training:* all-round exercises, orientated to special type of sport (not all-round and general);
  - *Build-up and Advanced Build-up Training:* all-round exercises, orientated to special type of sport and purely specific exercises;
  - *High Performance Training:* purely specific exercises:

- Speed exercises carried out at *sub-maximal speed* create sub-maximal speed movement patterns in the brain, instead of maximal ones; consequently slower movements are "learnt".

23

- One is truly fast when one can "play" with high speeds, i.e. can control and feel movements, and can *"sense" speed variations.*
- In speed training, the *repetition method* is mainly used. Characteristics of this method are:
- All exercises are carried out at *maximal* and/or *supra maximal* movement speed e.g. under body weight-reducing conditions, or with equipment for reducing bodyweight, or under so-called forced conditions;
- the *concentration* of the athlete should be focused completely on the speed of the movement and only "incidentally" on the technique itself;
- the exercises should not be carried out under *signs of fatigue* - their quantity and duration are dependent on age, state of fitness and type of training;
- maximal movement speed should be practised one to three times a week, each time with a *variety of exercises*, to avoid signs of neural fatigue (after one "maximal" speed training unit the body requires about 72 hours to recover fully), and to avoid neural stabilisation, which could lead to a so-called coordination or speed barrier i.e. after a few weeks of constantly identical training stimuli there is no more adaptation of the central nervous system.

4.2 "LEARNING" AND TRAINING OF TIME-PROGRAMMES

4.2.1 DEFINITION AND METHODICAL HINTS

By *Time-programmes* we mean the elementary movement patterns (-programmes) which are stored and trained in the brain and which are connected to a middle level by means of the patterning of the nerve conducting speed, muscle self reflex and muscle fibre structure. They work unconsciously, as they should require less time than 170ms.

Their development obviously affects a connection between the learning storing processes in the brain and an increase in the reactive tension abilities (stretch-shortening cycle) in the muscle-tendon tissue (c.f. also page 16).

In the exercises which follow, exact *methodical instructions* are given. In general, in the training of time-programmes, it is true that all exercises must be carried out at maximal or supra maximal speed, and the recovery between exercises or series should always be complete.

The *methodical procedure* consists of:	
Intensity:	maximal without unloading; supra maximal with unloading
Repetitions:	6-8 times, 2-4 series (sets)
Rest between sets:	2-5 minutes
Periodisation:	1-3 training units (TU) per week or 1-2 times parallel with frequency and action velocity training -6 weeks in Autumn and -2 times 4 weeks in the period January - May.
Training exercises:	see the exercises presented below

4.2.2 EXERCISES TO FORM TIME-PROGRAMMES BY JUMPS

Drop ("box") Jump

Exercise 1

The player stands on a raised surface of 20-40cm. He carries out a drop-jump, followed by a maximally fast, flat take-off.

Attention should be paid to pre-tensing the calf muscles, only a very slight knee bend in the support phase, no touching of the floor with the heels, and body tension.

Variations:
Exercise as above, but carried out with added unloading.
Training equipment: belt, harness held at the hips.

Programme:
6-8 repetitions after 5-10 seconds
2-4 series
2-5 minutes rest

Important
- Coach encourages with metaphors, e.g. "bounce like a rubber ball"
- the arms are initially not used as swing elements, then actively engaged
- players must concentrate completely.

Exercise 2 — Rope Skipping

The player skips at maximal speed. He jumps only on the balls of the feet, without bending the knees, without the heels touching the floor and with optimal body tension.

Variations:
double jumps (two turns of the rope per jump)

> *Programme:*
> 6-10 seconds or 1 x 15 - 20 repetitions
> 2-4 series
> 2 - 5 minutes rest

Exercise 3 — Foot Tapping

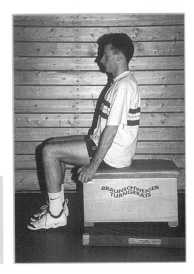

The player stands with his body tensed. The body's centre of mass is low and the player alternately raises and lowers his left and right foot balls, keeping the ankles rigid. The tempo is maximal/as fast as possible.

Variations:
Exercise in a lying or seated position.

> *Programme:*
> 5-8 seconds
> 2-4 series
> 2-5 min rest

4.2.3 EXERCISES TO FORM TIME-PROGRAMMES BY THROWING

Exercise 1 ———————————————————— Reactive throws

The player sits in an upright position with the back supported. The coach throws balls of different weights at high speed to him. The player throws back the balls reactively with a maximal short backswing movement.

Variations:
Exercises can be carried out with one arm.
The player throws the ball with an own backswing movement.

Programme:
6-8 repetitions
2-4 series
2-5 min rest

Exercise 2 ———————————————————— Hand tapping

The player sits or kneels in front of a raised surface, e.g. a stool, a box, a table, etc., and hits lightly with the palm of the hand with a tensed forearm as fast as possible on the surface. The hands can also move backwards and forwards or cross over.

Programme:
5-8 seconds
2-4 series
1-3 min rest

4.2.4 EXERCISES TO FORM TIME-PROGRAMMES BY SERVICES

Exercise 1

Reactive serves

The player kneels on both knees. The back swing movement is carried out with a short swing over the shoulder. Care should be taken that the upper body and shoulder area remain as still as possible, and that the swing is only carried out by the lower arm and wrist.

For small children, as the racquet size corresponding to their age can be too heavy, a much lighter racquet is recommended.

With increasing technical improvement the weight of the racquet can be increased.

Programme:
4-8 repetitions
2-4 series
2-5 min rest

4.3 — TRAINING OF REACTION SPEED AND ACTION VELOCITY

4.3.1 DEFINITION AND METHODICAL HINTS

By *reaction speed* we mean the ability to react to a stimulus as fast as possible, and by *action velocity*, we mean the ability to carry out acyclical movements at high speed against low external resistance.

Both forms of movement are always closely connected in tennis e.g. acting at the net, for one calls on the fast actions of the processing procedure in the brain (=stimulus processing), and the other calls on the necessary muscles (=muscle contractions) for the strokes concerned. In the practical game top speed actions are partially dependent on a good speed strength base, so that a sharp division between "pure" action speed (also only against low external resistance), and speed strength or strength speed, is often not possible; the boundaries are blurred.

- The following *training exercises*, however, should be carried out at maximum speed, as far as possible against very low external resistance.
- The *improvement of reaction speed* is mainly related to tennis-specific (partial) movements; i.e. in connection with technique or technique-related training. Furthermore, anticipation ability plays a crucial role.
- In the *improvement of action speed* either already formed (existing) time-programmes are integrated into specific movements/exercises, or specific acyclical movements are formed at the required speed (maximal/supra maximal) for the formation of short time-programmes. If tennis-specific technique is called on in training exercises, then consequently it is a question of a combined speed-technique training.

A precondition of the improvement of action speed is thus the *mastery of movement technique* i.e. well-trained inter muscular coordination. If this is not given, the corresponding technique must initially be trained and patterned at medium and sub maximal speeds.

Training Methods to improve reaction speed in conjunction with tennis-specific Action velocity

Intensity:	maximal movement velocity
Volume:	maximum of 8 seconds or 8-15 repetitions
Series:	3-5; rest between series: 2-3 min
Periodisation:	in every technique training unit, year round
Training exercises:	all technique-specific games with reaction components (esp. at the net). See exercises presented below.

Training Methods to improve action velocity

Intensity:	maximal/supra maximal
Volume:	see each exercise
Series:	3-5; rest between series; 2-3 mins
Variations:	By maximal/supra maximal intensity, by choice of exercise, by reduction of space and time in which exercise is carried out.
Training units per week:	1-3 each time as part of a training unit
Annual periodisation:	4-6 weeks training, then 1-3 months rest, then once more 3-5 weeks training, and so on.
Training exercises:	Technique (partial) movements, imitation movements, competition movements See the exercises presented below

4.3.2 EXERCISES TO IMPROVE REACTION SPEED AND ACTION VELOCITY WITHOUT ANTICIPATION

Exercise 1

Fast Blocking 1

Player stands at a distance of about 1.5m in front of a wall, the coach about 1m behind him. Both face the wall. The coach now throws balls in rapid succession against the wall, the player blocks the rebounding balls or hits them away.

Variations:
The coach throws the balls fast or slowly
- at different heights
- with bounce on the floor
- via a corner

Player: blocks only with the hands
- only with the feet
- situational blocking (foot-body - or hand blocking)

Programme:
8-15 repetitions
3-8 series
2-3 minutes rest

Important:
The degree of difficulty of the exercise should be such that the player cannot get 25% of the balls

Exercise 2

Fast Blocking 2

Player lies on his back with arms and legs in the air. Coach stands on a box and drops balls onto the player. Player tries to block or hit away the balls with fastest possible blocking movements.

Variations:
Coach throws in different directions and verbally encourages the player.

Programme:
10-20 repetitions
3-8 series and more
2-3 minutes rest

Exercise 3

Fast Blocking 3

Three players stand in a row, about 2-4m apart. The middle player looks at one of the outside players. The outside players have 4-6 balls each. The middle player receives a ball at high speed in conjunction with an acoustic signal. He blocks this ball. He then turns quickly towards the other player, who quickly throws another ball to him, etc. Players change places after 10-15 throws.

Variations:
• distances between the players are changed
• player blocks with different parts of the body

Programme:
10-15 repetitions
3-5 series
2-3 minutes rest

Exercise 4

Goalkeeper training

Three to five players stand in a row looking at the blocking player. They have 2-3 balls each and throw in a pre-set order to the blocking player, who does not know this order. The throwers swing the ball back at the same time, only one throws, and so on in the pre-set order. The blocking player blocks the balls.

Variations:
• constantly change the throwing order.

Programme:
5-15 repetitions
3-5 series
2-3 minutes rest

Exercise 5

Goal throws

One player, a thrower, jumps above a vertically positioned soft mat or other obstacle and throws a ball over this obstacle towards the goal. The goal keeper must block. The throwing player must either be seen as late as possible or not at all by the goalkeeper.

Programme:
3-6 repetitions
3-5 series
2-4 minutes rest.

Variations:
Player can also throw around the side of the obstacle.

NB: rests can also be a little longer as this exercise presents a high jumping strength load for the throwing player.

Exercise 6

Catching, hitting away

The coach stands in front of the baseline, several tennis balls in each hand. The coach drops a ball, the player must either catch or hit away this ball and then return to the starting point.

Variations:
* Distances between coach and player can be increased.
* At greater distances the ball should also bounce once or twice.

Programme:
8-15 repetitions
3-5 series
2-3 minutes rest

Important:
Success rate/degree of difficulty should be set at about 60%. 40% of the balls thrown should not be returnable by the player (to avoid a speed barrier).

Fast catching

Exercise 7

The coach stands behind the player and throws a ball forwards over the player's head. The player has the task of catching the ball directly, after it has bounced once, or at most twice. The player's centre of mass is low and he moves on the balls of the feet.

Variations:
- coach gives an additional acoustic signal.
- player must only start when both signals have been given.

Programme:
8-15 repetitions
3-5 series
2-3 minutes rest

Catching Game Day and Night or Black and White

Exercise 8

Two players lie or stand opposite each other. There should be sufficient distance between them. Each player has a code word/number. When the coach calls out the code word, the player concerned must catch or touch the other player. Then the body positions can be changed, the distance between the players can be changed, and the code word can be changed. The players run in different directions.

Programme:
3-6 repetitions
15 seconds rest
3-5 series
1-3 minutes rest

Exercise 9 — Catching Numbers

Two players get a number each (e.g. 1 and 7). The players move in free or controlled movement forms (running, hopping, side-step) in a pre-determined space. On a command, the player whose number is called out must catch, or touch the other player. The players' centre of mass is low and they move mainly on the balls of the feet.

Variations:
- dribbling the ball
- fast change of numbers
- the size of the space used can be changed (service area).

Programme:
variable duration of stimulus, not longer than 10-15 seconds.
3-5 series
2-3 minutes rest

Exercise 10 — Shadow running

One player makes free or controlled movements, the other players must quickly copy the movements. The distance to player 1 must be maintained. The tasks change after one/two repetitions. The players keep their body centre of gravity low and work as fast as possible.

Variations:
- establish space limits
- establish combinations of movement forms, or work spontaneously
- the players can be joined together with a cord which must not break.

Programme:
maximum 8-12 seconds
3-5 repetitions
2-3 minutes rest

37

Sprints

Exercise 11

The player carries out short sprints on a visual, acoustic or tactile signal. These should be in different directions, and should be carried out as fast as possible.

Variations:
The start can also be carried out from:
- the basic position with low centre of gravity
- a split-step
- skipping, ankling or tapping

Programme:
3-4 times 3-5 minutes - maximum up to 6 seconds (rest 8-10 seconds)
3-5 series
2-3 minutes rest

"Sensory Method" (Training of Time Perception)

Exercise 12

The player sprints a fixed distance on a signal. He receives information from the coach about the scored time. Repetitions at least 2-3x. The time needed for the next repetitions must be estimated by the player himself. If this is well estimated, the player should complete the set distance at the estimated speed.

Programme:
3 repetitions, 10 seconds each rest = 1 series
3-5 series
2-3 minutes rest
maximum duration of stimulus 8 seconds

Variations:
Change type of movement (e.g. side-step)

Small Games

Exercise 13

1. "Foot touching"

Players stand in front of each other, taken by the hands or hands behind their backs. They try to step on each others' feet (only touching them).

Programme:
5-8 seconds
3-5 series
2-3 minutes rest

2."Thigh slapping"

Starting position as for number 1. The players hit each other on the outside of the thigh (touching).

Programme:
8- a maximum of 10 seconds
3-5 series
2-3 minutes rest.

Touch or hit all kinds of balls with the racquet

Exercise 14

Carry out exercises 6 and 7 with a racquet, trying to play the ball as a half-volley. A half-volley requires not only reaction and action speed but also starting strength, and the quality of the execution and the exercise management can be judged much better.

Programme:
10-15 repetitions
3-5 series
2-3 minutes rest

Exercise 15

Touch and block balls with the racquet

The player stands about 1-1.5m from a wall, facing it. The coach stands about 1-3m behind him and throws balls against the wall (possibly via the corners). The player must try to touch the thrown ball with the racquet.

Programme:
10-15 repetitions
3-5 series
2-3 minutes rest

Exercise 16

Deceptive Volleys

The coach stands near the net and plays the ball from the hand to the player on the other side of the net. In the process, he tries to deceive the player by the way he moves his wrist. The player must try to touch the ball, later to volley it.

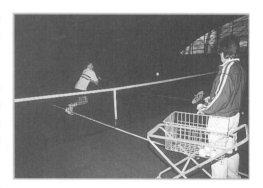

Programme:
10-15 repetitions
3-5 series
1.5-2 minutes rest

Exercise 17

Machine gun at the net

The coach stands near the net and plays about 10 balls in very quick succession in different directions to the player on the other side of the net, who must try to touch all balls and later to volley them.

Programme:
10 repetitions
3 series
2-3 minutes rest

Exercise 18

Shooting at the net

The coach stands near the net, the player stands just in front of the t-line on the other side of the net. The coach feeds balls very fast straight at the player's body and tries to hit him. The player must try to block the oncoming balls with his racquet. Care should be taken that the coach feeds the balls mainly at hip height, not at head height, to avoid possible injury. The player should not move backwards.

Programme:
10 repetitions
3 series
2-3 minutes rest

Exercise 19

Volley duel at the net

One player stands on one side of the net and two players stand quite near each other on the other side all playing volleys. For the two players anticipation is hardly possible as they cannot predict to which one of them the ball will be played at.

After 3-5 series the players should change places.

Programme:
10-15 repetitions
3-5 series
2-3 minutes rest

Exercise 20

Service to net player

Two players stand at the net; one, two or three players are on the other side of the net behind the baseline. These players alternately hit a first service from the centre of the baseline to the players at the net, whereby they should "shoot at" each of the net players, in no particular order, in order to eliminate anticipation. Young players can stand further in the court to serve. The net players must try to touch the balls, later to volley them, without turning or moving backwards. Care should be taken that the net players stand on the balls of the feets, and move forwards when the server hits the ball.

Programme:
10-15 services per player
3-5 series
2-3 minutes rest

Exercise 21

Volley Lob and Smash

Four players stand in doubles formation at the net. The coach feeds a ball to one pair, which plays a flat volley. The other side plays a volley lob back, which should not be too long. The first side must smash and the others must then try to get this smash, without turning or moving backwards.

Programme:
15-20 smashes
3 series
2-3 minutes rest (side change)

Wave attack

Exercise 22

Two players stand on the base line, two at the net. The coach feeds the balls to the baseline players. They must approach with an attacking ball. The rally is played with volleys. In this exercise it is recommended that six to eight players stand in pairs behind the baseline to keep the game going. If the attacking players make a mistake, they always move outwards and backwards, and the coach can immediately play to the next pair waiting.

Programme:
10-15 rallies, then change sides
3-5 series
2-3 minutes rest.

4.3.3 EXERCISES TO IMPROVE REACTION SPEED AND ACTION VELOCITY WITH ANTICIPATION

Passing shots against net players

Exercise 1

One player stands at the baseline, the other at the net. The coach plays to the net player, who should play a long volley. The baseline player must try to pass the net player, the rally should be played out to the end.

Programme:
5-10 rallies, then change sides
3-5 series
2-3 minutes rest

Lobs and Smashes

Exercise 2

One player stands at the net the other at the baseline. The coach plays to the net player, who plays a long volley. The baseline player plays only lobs from now on, the net player tries to smash winners, the baseline player tries to reach them.

Programme:
10 rallies, then change sides
3-5 series
2-3 minutes rest

Exercise 3 ——————————————— Service and Return

One player serves, the other returns. In order to make the exercise more difficult and emphasise reaction speed even more, the ball can be served over a shorter distance (e.g. from up to behind the t-line), or returned from a shorter distance in front of the baseline.

Programme:
20-30 services, then change sides
3-5 series
2-3 minutes rest

Exercise 4 ——————————————— Serve and Volley

One player serves and volleys, the other returns and tries to pass him. Points are played out to the end.

Programme:
20-30 serves, then change sides
3-5 series
2 minutes rest

Exercise 5 ——————————————— Volley Duel two against two

All four players stand at the net. The coach starts off, and the point is played out with volleys.

Programme:
10-15 duels
3-5 series
2-3 minutes rest

**Exercises for Reaction and action speed
with added perception and anticipation**

Exercise 6

One player stands on either side of the court, one at the net and the other at the baseline. The coach starts playing to the baseline player. The net player must react correctly, according to the body movement and the point of contact of the baseline player, in doing so both players know how the baseline player should react. This could be organised as follows:

Long ball:
• the baseline player must run backwards, then play a passing shot always only down the line.

Short ball:
• the baseline player runs forwards and plays:
• a passing shot down the line from a high point of contact,
• a passing shot across court from a low point of contact.

Medium length ball:
• the baseline player plays a passing shot down the line by making a big turn for the back swing,
• plays the ball across court after turning the body slightly,

• a late point of contact produces a ball down the line,
• if the ball is hit at its highest point it will go down the line,
• if the ball is hit low it will go across court.

Ball to the body:
• the baseline player is in a lean back and plays a forehand to the backhand of the net player.

According to position of the net player:
• if the net player is still standing on the left side of the court the ball is played to his forehand side, if he is standing on the right it will be played to his back hand.

The additional exercises above all deal with the reaction training of the baseline player. He must try to "read" (i.e. anticipate) the behaviour of the net player, and react accordingly. The net player should play volleys according to a set pattern:

• for a ball which should land on the side of the net player between the t-line and the baseline, he always plays a long volley,

- for a ball which should bounce in the service area, the net player always plays a short cross-court shot,
- for a very short ball, the net player plays a drop volley.

Of course, all other possible variations can be used. It is important that the player who must react always knows what to look out for, and that the other player adopts the corresponding behaviour patterns.

TRAINING OF FREQUENCY SPEED

4.4

4.4.1 DEFINITION AND METHODICAL HINTS

Frequency speed means the ability to carry out cyclical movements e.g. tappings, short sprints, at highest possible speed against low external resistance.

In sport - as for action speed - fastest possible cyclic movements are partially dependent on a good speed strength/strength speed base, so that a clear division between "pure" frequency speed (therefore only against low external resistance), and strength speed is often not possible.

- The following *training exercises* should, however, be carried out for the maximum improvement of cyclic speed movements, if possible against very low external resistance, and always at maximal intensity (speed).

- For the *improvement of frequency speed* either available time-programmes are integrated into certain movements/exercises, or certain cyclic movements are trained at the speed necessary for the formation of short time-programmes.

If tennis-specific techniques are used as training exercises, it is a question of combined speed-technique training.

A pre-condition for the improvement of frequency speed is consequently a *mastery of movement technique* (well-trained inter muscular coordination). Should this not be given, the corresponding technique must initially be formed at medium and sub-maximal speeds.

Hint:
Further and detailed presentations of the training of action velocity and frequency speed can be found in Grosser (1991).

Training Methods to improve frequency speed

Intensity:	maximal/supra maximal
Repetitions:	4-12
Series:	3-4 (maximal altogether 20 repetitions)
Rest between series:	2-10 minutes
Variations:	by intensity maximal/supra maximal, by choice of exercise, by duration.

Methodical tip: All exercises for frequency speed should also be trained with the methods of the delay-effect phenomenon (see: speed barrier/delay-effect)

Equipment:	weighted vest, wrist weights, trampette, soft mats, ropes, etc.
NB:	*The increased level of effort requires a long rest between series, possibly a shortening of the duration and amount of stimulus.*
	Pay increased attention to the quality of the movement!
Planning:	e.g. 1-2 with load or 2-5 x normal, 3-5 series, 2-5 minutes rest.
Important:	*all exercises for frequency speed should also be trained from the point of view of body weight unloading – supra maximally.*
	Equipment: declined running track, pulling rope, etc.
	Supra maximal execution speed produces great fatigue. Shorten stimulus duration, lengthen rests, decrease stimulus volume. The coach should look out for optimal coordination of the partial impulse!
Training units per week:	1-3 (each as part of a training unit)
Year periodisation:	4-6 weeks training, 1-3 months rest, then again 3-5 weeks training, etc.

4.4.2 EXERCISES TO IMPROVE FREQUENCY SPEED WITH FOCUS ON LEGS

Exercise 1

Foot tapping

The player stands in starting position with a low centre of gravity and with the body in tension, and alternately raises and lowers the ball of the right and left feet with a rigid ankle. The speed should be maximal/as fast as possible.

Variations:
Carry out the exercise in a lying or sitting position.

Programme:
5-8 seconds
3-5 series
2-4 minutes rest

Exercise 2

Ankling

The player stands upright, un-supported or leaning against some-thing, and alternately raises and lowers the heels.

Points to watch: the body should be in tension, the centre of mass should be high, the foot contact should be active/reactive. Should be carried out as fast as possible.

Variations:
- working tempo can be varied, fast - slow
- with or without touching down with the heel
- carry out the exercise with (weighted vest, weight etc.) delay-effect phenomenon.

Programme:
5-8 seconds
3-5 series
2-3 minutes rest

with delay-effect phenomenon:
3-6 seconds
2-4 series
with 2-4 minutes rest

Important: fault correction:
- no clear shift of balance
- knee-lift too high/too low

Exercise 3
Skipping

The player stands in basic position and alternately raises and lowers both legs with medium or high knee lift. The arms swing "naturally bent", the legs are bent and straightened as fast as possible, the support leg must always be straight, the upper body is upright.

Variations:
- skipping with only medium knee lift, or only with high knee lift, or both combined.
- moving forwards or on the spot.

Programme:
5-8 seconds
3-8 series
2-5 minutes rest

Exercise 4
High knee running

The player stands in the starting position. The feet are hip-width apart, the upper body is upright. The player alternately raises and lowers both legs.

The knee of the swing leg must be lifted above the horizontal level when raised. The legs are bent and straightened as fast as possible and the support leg is always straight.

Programme:
3-8 or 4-6 repetitions per leg
3-8 series
2-5 minutes rest

Exercise 5

Movement combinations of exercises
4.4.2.1 - 4.4.2.2 - 4.4.2.3 and 4.4.2.4

Programme:
4-8 seconds
2-4 series
2-5 minutes rest

Important:
Two, or maximally three movement elements in one combination.
• Optimally streched knee muscules are a precondition for a high quality execution.

Stretching by exercises 4.6.4.2, no. 10-13, 18-19.

Exercise 6

Heel Kicks

The player alternately bends the knees and kicks his/her bottom with the heels. The knees remain below the body's centre of mass, the upper body is upright. The target movement can also start with foot tapping or ankling. The knee extending muscles should be optimally streched. (Exercises: 4.6.4.2, No. 12,19, 24).

Variations:
• player hangs from rings, horizontal bar, etc.
• player lies in prone position
• in the basic exercise the hands hit the heels.

Programme:
5-8 seconds or 3-5 x each leg
3-6 series
2-3 minutes rest

Exercise 7

Leg crossing in front and behind

The player moves the right leg to the left, crossing in front of the left leg; the left leg moves behind, etc., and vice versa. Body weight should be on the balls of the feet and the body should be in tension.

Variations:
- only right leg in front of left leg
- only left leg in front of right leg
- the right leg is placed alternately in front of and behind the left leg
- the left leg is placed alternately in front of and behind the right leg.

Programme:
5-8 seconds
3-8 series
2-4 minutes rest

Exercise 8

Side-step

The player stands in basic position, feet hip-width apart, upper body upright.

One leg (right or left) is moved out to the side, the other leg is moved behind as fast as possible. The direction of movement can be changed, the stride length can be changed, or pre-set by markings.

Programme:
5-8 seconds
5-10 series
1-3 minutes rest

Important:
The adductor, abductor and gluteal muscles should be optimally streched.

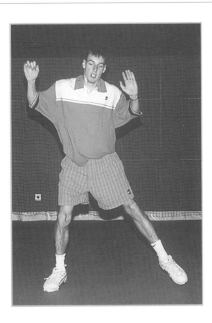

From all exercises focusing on frequency speed of the legs, movement combinations should be built up

Exercise 9

The following should be noted:

Programme:
maximum 8 seconds
3-8 series
2-4 minutes rest
Stimulus intensity as fast as possible.

- do not combine more than two exercises. If there is a visible loss of speed, stimulus duration should be shortened.
- the changing of elements can take place on an acoustic or visual signal.

Streching:
Exercises 4.6.4.2, no. 12-16 and 19.

Exercise 10

Pendulum

From a square of about 30 x 30 or 20 x 20 cm, the player places, e.g. his right foot to the left (crossing) and back again, subsequently reversed. The body's centre of mass is low (see picture), the balls of the feet are actively plant. The movements can also be backwards and forwards.

Programme:
5-8 seconds
3-5 series
2-4 minutes rest

Magic Triangle

Exercise 11

The player moves the feet as fast as possible in different directions outside and inside the triangle. Backwards and forwards movement should also be encouraged.

Programme:
4-8 seconds,
3-5 series,
2-4 minutes rest

Important:
The obstacles should be low, maximum 8-12cm high. One bar should be left loose (to reduce risk of injury).

Exercise 12 — Ladder run

The player covers a ladder lying on the ground in different ways as fast as possible (hitting each space between the rungs of the ladder). Only the balls of the feet should touch the ground, the body's centre of mass is low, the knees are slightly bent.

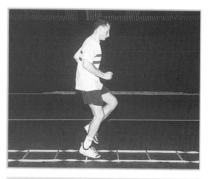

Variations:
- one foot per ladder space
- one foot after the other in the same space
- run backwards over the ladder. Forwards and backwards combinations
- sideways run - one foot in each space
- sideways run with leg-crossing, e.g. right in front of left and vice versa,
- sideways running the left leg
- leg crossing, e.g. right in front of and behind left, and vice versa.

Programme:
according to the length of the ladder, not more than
5-8 seconds
3-5 series
2-4 minutes rest

Important:
The learning of a new movement combination (pattern/rhythm) should also be at a slow speed.

Exercise 13 — Short sprint on sloping track (reduction of body weight)

The player sprints from a standing position or a short run-up downhill on a sloping track. The upper body is upright, the movement carried out on the balls of the feet.

Programme:
2-6 x 8-12m. In between a rest of 10-15 seconds = 1 series
3-5 series
2-5 minutes rest

Exercise 14 — Side-step on sloping track (reduction of body weight)

The player carries out side-steps downhill on a sloping track. The upper body is upright, the body's centre of mass is lowered.

Programme:
2-4 x 6-8 m. In between a rest of about 10 - 15 seconds = 1 series
3-5 series
2-5 minutes rest between series

Exercise 15 — Leg work with counter resistance

The player is linked to the coach by an elastic rope. The player moves away from the coach (e.g. backwards run) and, on a signal from the coach with the support of the elastic rope, sprints towards the coach.

Variations:
- the player runs away backwards and sprints forwards
- the player side-steps away from the coach to the left or right and then side-steps back to the coach
- the player runs away forwards and sprints backwards towards the coach.

Programme:
2-4 x, rest in between about 10-15 seconds = 1 series
3-6 series
2-4 minutes rest

Important:
The maximal movement speed can initially cause problems in the movement flow. The quality of movement should therefore first be ensured by repeated *practice.*

4.4.3 EXERCISES TO IMPROVE FREQUENCY SPEED WITH FOCUS ON SHOULDERS/ARMS

Fast Boxing movements

Exercise 1

The player kneels or sits and carries out boxing movements at the highest possible movement frequency. The upper body is still, abdominal and back muscles are tensed.

Variations:
Movement can be a straight punch, a hook, or an uppercut.

> ***Programme:***
> 5-6 seconds
> 3-5 series
> 2-4 minutes rest

Hand-tapping

Exercise 2

The player sits or kneels in front of a raised surface, e.g. stool, box, table, etc. and hits the palm of the hand as fast as possible on the surface with the forearm tensed. The movement can also be backwards and forwards, the hands can also cross.

> ***Programme***
> 5-8 seconds
> 3-6 series
> 2-3 minutes rest

NB: The exercises can also be carried out with additional delay-effect phenomenon. Equipment: wrist weights, small dumbbells, boxing gloves which produces good delay-effect.

Exercise 3 ——————— Fast Throwing Serves

The player sits or kneels and throws balls forwards as fast and as frequently as possible, also with great aiming accuracy.

The throwing heights are: shoulder level – higher than shoulder level – hip level. The balls (tennis balls, throwing balls 50-200g) should be readily available.

Programme:
6-10 repetitions
3-5 series
2-3 minutes rest

Exercise 4 ——————— As above but with delay-effect by medicine ball throwing (1-3kg)

Programme:
1-3 medicine ball throws,
5-6 "normal" throws = 1 series
3-5 series
2-3 minutes rest

NB: Exercises 3 and 4 are also to be carried out with the "wrong" (non favourite) arm.

Exercise 5

Service in combination with throws. Delay-effect phenomenon

The player first throws with a tennis ball or a rounders ball (should weigh from 80 up to 200g) about 10-15 times as far and as fast as possible. Directly afterwards he serves 6-12 first serves with the tennis racquet (about 300g), also at maximum speed. Due to the lower weight of the ball the arm movement is greatly accelerated. This effect, which is recorded and stored by the central nervous system (delay-effect), is carried directly over into the racquet swing, so that this is faster than usual.

Programme:
10-15 throws + 6-12 serves
3-5 series
1-3 minutes rest

Exercise 6

Service in combination with medicine ball throws

The player initially throws about 6-10 times with a medicine ball, weighing between 0.5 and 1kg for fit up and coming players, as far and high as possible, roughly imitating the movement of the service. Directly afterwards he hits 8-10 first serves as fast as possible. The delay-effect phenomenon also works here, but this time in reverse. The central nervous system has adjusted to the relatively high resistance provided by the heavier weight of the medicine ball. This is not given when the tennis racquet is used. Therefore, the racquet is automatically accelerated more than usual.

Programme:
1-6 medicine ball throws +
8-10 serves = 1 series
3-5 series
2-3 minutes rest

Exercise 7

Frequency speed with racquet

The player stands on the baseline, the coach at the net. The latter plays the balls in quick succession with a curved lob to one side of the player. The player must try to get to all balls and return them, hitting them just before the second bounce.

Programme:
10 repetitions
3-5 series
2-3 minutes rest

COMBINED TRAINING OF ACTION VELOCITY, FREQUENCY SPEED, STRENGTH-SPEED AND COORDINATIVE ABILITIES

4.5

4.5.1 DEFINITION AND METHODICAL HINTS

The following exercise examples are for the *multiple improvement of speed abilities* and selected *coordination abilities*. The latter comprises so-called performance pre-conditions for improved learning or execution of technique-specific movements. Examples of coordination abilities: balance, spatial and temporal orientation, kinaesthetic differenciation (feeling for movement).

Such exercises should however first be used when the separate speed abilities have already been practised in isolation.

In addition to this training, in most cases, the strength and endurance abilities and corresponding flexibility exercises shown in Chapter 4.6 must be trained.

Training methods to improve combined speed abilities

Intensity: maximum

Volume/Duration
of exercises: 9-12 years 5 seconds
                    13-16 years 6-7 seconds
                    from 16:17 years, 6-10 seconds or 4-10 repetitions

rest between repetitions: 2-3 minutes

Training units per week: 2

Periodisation: 4-8 weeks training (at least 12 training units),
                    then 2-4 weeks rest, etc.

Training exercises: see exercises shown in 4.5.2

4.5.2 EXERCISES FOR THE COMBINED IMPROVEMENT OF ACTION VELOCITY, FREQUENCY SPEED, STRENGTH-SPEED AND CO-ORDINATIVE ABILITIES

Exercise 1 ────────────── Combination sprint 1

The player carries out the exercises in the following order:

Jumping jacks - side-steps to 2, sprint forwards to 3, sprint forwards to 4, sprint backwards to 3 and backwards jump to 1 with fastest possible movement speed. Body's centre of mass is low, the load is transferred to the balls of the feet.

Programme:
Jumping jacks 2-5 x
Running distance 3-5m
backwards sprint
3-5m = 1 series
3-8 series
2-4 minutes rest

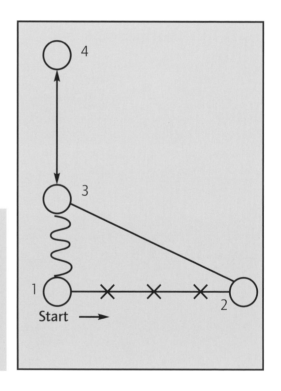

Exercise 2

Combination sprint 2

The player stands on one or both legs on a therapy spinning top, medicine ball or on climbing blocks. The player carries out the following exercises in this order:

>balancing, low centre of mass, upper body upright> depth jump> reactive jump over obstacle 2 (10-

30cm) > sprint forwards to 3 > side-steps to 4 > sprint backwards to 1.

The movement execution has to be as fast as possible, the coach checks that the balls of the feet are used and the body carriage is upright. (> = next exercise).

Programme:
balancing 4-8 seconds
sprinting distance 3-5m
3-5 series
2-4 minutes rest

Exercise 3

Combination sprint 3

The player moves with a "pedalo" 2-3 x forwards/backwards over a distance of 1-3m (1), then carries out a depth jump with immediate reactive take-off over a small obstacle (2) (10-20cm) > side-steps to 3 > sprint forwards to 4 > side-steps to 5 > backwards sprint to 6. Performance as fast as possible, body's centre of mass low, and on the balls of the feet.

Programme:
Jumping jacks 2-5 x
Running distance 3-5m
backwards sprint 3-5m
= 1 series
3-8 series
2-4 minutes rest

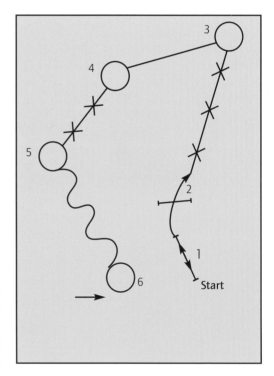

Variations:

Exercises 1-3 - the end points can be touched with one hand at a time. Exercises can also be carried out as competitions.

Exercise 4

Fan-like run 1

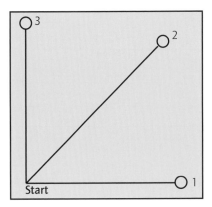

The player moves as fast as possible between the start and finish marks. The body's centre of mass is low, the running should be on the balls of the feet. Body carriage is upright.

From the start > 1- forwards, back to the start sideways
From the start > 2 forwards, back to the start forwards
From the start > 3 forwards, back to the start backwards.

Programme:
2-4 repetitions with
10-20 seconds rest
2-5 series
2-5 minutes rest

Exercise 5

Fan-like run 2

As fan-like run 1, only to the other side. Movement and planning as in exercise 4.

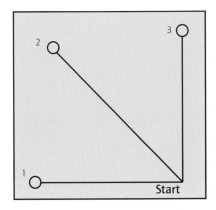

Exercise 6

Order of running direction and type of movement:
Start to 1 sideways, back to the start sideways
Start to 2 forwards, back to the start backwards
Start to 3 forwards, back to the start sideways
Planning: as in Fan-like run 1.

Fan-like run 3

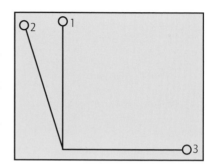

Exercise 7

Start to 1 forwards, back to start backwards
Start to 2 forwards, back to start sideways
Start to 3 forwards, back to start forwards
Programme: as in Fan-like run 1.

Fan-like run 4

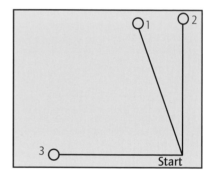

Exercise 8

Start to 1 forwards, back to start sideways
Start to 2 forwards, back to start backwards
Start to 3 forwards, back to start sideways.

Fan-like run 5

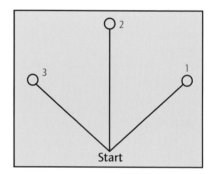

Exercise 9

Complete Fan-like Run
(length of running distance about 2-4m)

The player moves as fast as possible between the start and finish marks. The body's centre of mass is low, running should be on the balls of the feet. Body posture is upright.

Running order:

Start to 1 forwards, back to start forwards
Start to 2 forwards, back to start sideways

Start to 3 forwards, back to start backwards
Start to 4 forwards, back to start sideways
Start to 5 forwards, back to start forwards

Programme:
2-4 repetitions with 1 minute rest
3-4 series
2-5 minutes rest

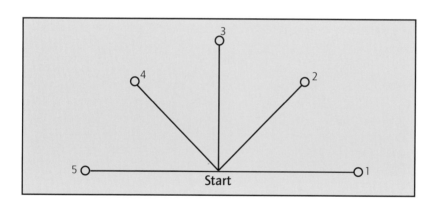

Exercise 10

Tennis court exercise

The player sprints set distance at highest possible speed.

Programme:
2 repetitions with
1 minute rest
2-4 series
2-5 minutes rest

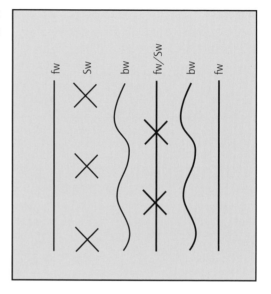

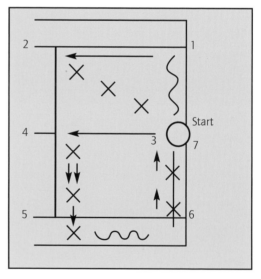

Exercise 11

ZigZag runs

The player sprints set distance as fast as possible. The turning point has to be passed as fast as possible.

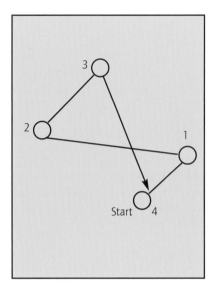

Programme:
As Exercise 10

Hints:
Variations:
- the end points of the running distance are touched with the hand or feet
- balls can be carried to and from the end points
- the start can be from basic position, from a split step, from tapping or from ankling
- the exercises can also be performed with the "delay-effect" with weighted vest
- different movements can be used (sideways, backwards, etc.).

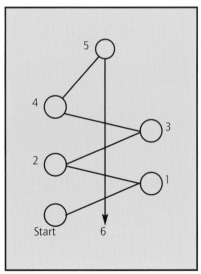

Exercise 12

The coach plays the ball from the net to set points so that the player can still reach them, and must return them with:
- half volley, or
- at the highest point of the bounce

In between he must always return to the centre of the baseline.

Programme:
Maximum intensity
5-10 seconds
3-5 series
2-3 minutes rest

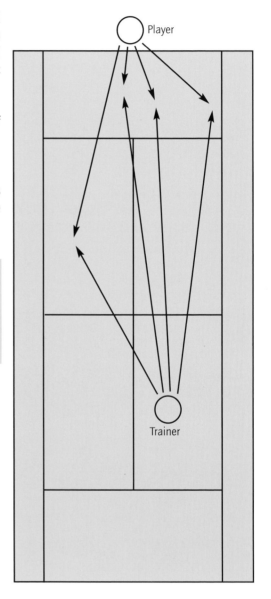

ZigZag runs with racquet

Player

Trainer

Exercise 13

Sprints with racquet and ball

The coach feeds balls from the net and basket in such a way that the player can only reach them after a maximal sprint. The balls should be hit with a slice (low bounce), flat, not too long (the player should run slightly diagonally forwards than diagonally backwards), and quite fast. The distance of the point of contact from the start position should be long enough so that the player can reach and hit 1/3 of the balls on the first bounce, can only manage to touch about another 1/3, and can touch the last 1/3 on the second bounce. It is a speed exercise and not a technique exercise. If the player cannot reach the ball on the first bounce, he should not give up and stop, but continue running and try to touch the ball.

A. Sprint over about 8-9m

B. Sprint over about 14m. Here the first ball must be played as a half-volley.

C. Sprint over about 18m

D. Sprint over about 24m

E. Sprint over about 26m

F. Sprint over about 32m

G. Sprint over about 46m

H. Sprint over about 55m

A. Sprint over about 8-9m

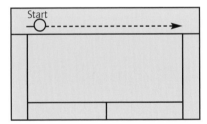

B. Sprint over about 14m.

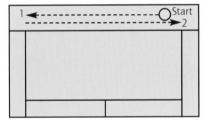

C. Sprint over about 18m

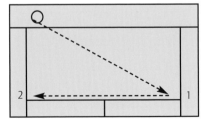

D. Sprint over about 24m

E. Sprint over about 26m

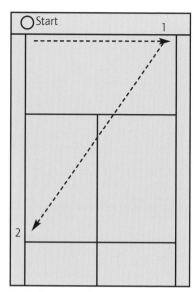

F. Sprint over about 32m

G. Sprint over about 46m

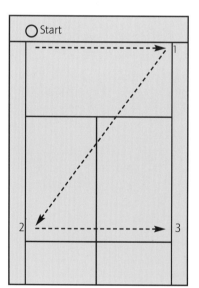

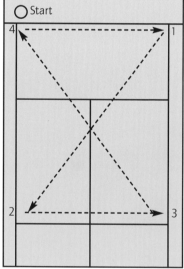

H. Sprint over about 55m

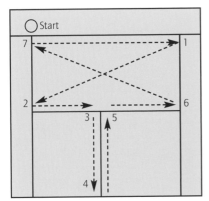

Programme:
Maximum Intensity.
Longer running distance requires
- shorter series and longer rest.

A group of 4-6 players is recommended, in order to get the
starting position for the next sprint
without rushing and without wasting
time.

Exercises A and B
4-6 repetitions
3 series
2 minutes rest

Exercise C:
3-5 repetitions
3 series
2 minutes rest

Exercises D and E:
3-4 repetitions
3 series
2-3 minutes rest

Exercise F:
2-4 repetitions
3 series
2-3 minutes rest

Exercise G:
2-3 repetitions
3 series
2-3 minutes rest

Exercise H:
1-2 repetitions
3 series
2-4 minutes rest

Points can be given for motivation:
- Hit on first bounce - 3 points
- Hit after second bounce with half-volley - 2 points
- Hit after second bounce - 1 point
- Hit after third bounce - no points

Exercise 14

Balancing exercises with racquet

The Coach hits balls to the player who is standing either on one leg, on a therapy spinning top or "pedalo", and volleys or smashes the ball back. As well two players can pass the balls to each other.

Programme:
10-15 repetitions
3-5 series
1-2 minute rest

Exercise 15

Fan-like runs with racquet

From the net the coach feeds three balls into the corners of the court, and in the corners of the sidelines and the t-line. The player must try to return all balls as half-volleys, and after every shot, run back to the centre of the baseline.

Programme:
2-3 repetitions
3 series
1-3 minutes rest

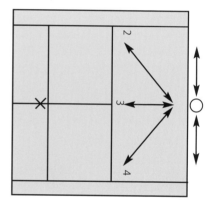

Exercise 16

Starting strength with tennis racquet I

From the net the coach hits the ball to between the t-line and the baseline, wide enough so that the player, standing behind the baseline, can only just reach it to volley it back.

Programme:
3-5 repetitions
3 series
1-2 minutes rest

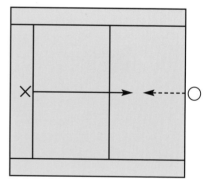

Exercise 17

Starting strength with tennis racquet II

From the net the coach hits the ball to between the t-line and the baseline so that the player, this time standing further behind the baseline, can only just reach the ball to half-volley it.

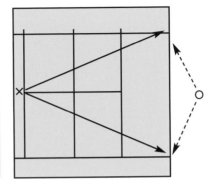

Programme:
3-5 repetitions
3 series
1-2 minutes rest

Exercise 18

Starting strength with tennis racquet III

The same exercise as in Exercise 17, except that the player must only hit the ball at the top of its bounces.

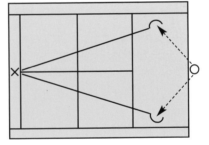

Programme:
3-5 repetitions
3 series
1-2 minutes rest

Exercise 19

Horizontal jumping strength at the net

The player stands near the net. From the other side of the net the coach hits balls to the left and right as far as the player can reach. He must take a short step into the ball with the near foot, and then a long jump with the other leg, reach the ball and volley it.

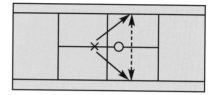

Programme:
6-10 repetitions
3 series
1-2 minutes rest

Exercise 20

Vertical jumping strength at the net

The player stands about 1-2m in front of the t-line. The coach lobs him so that the player can only just reach the ball with a double-footed jump from his basic stand. The player may not step backwards, he must try to take only one vertical jump from his basic stand to reach and smash the ball.

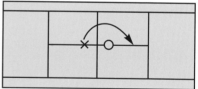

Programme:
5-10 repetitions
3 series
1-2 minutes rest

TRAINING OF COMPLEMENTARY PERFORMANCE-DETERMINING FACTORS
4.6

4.6.1 GENERAL COMMENTS

Based on our long practical experience with tennis-playing children, young people, national and international top players, we are of the opinion that speed, in its different forms, is the decisive athletic characteristic for overall tennis performance. Scientific findings support our theory. (cf. also our "Theses", page 9). As we have already stated, speed appears

- on the one hand in so-called *"pure" (elementary) forms (time-programmes, action and frequency speed)*, which must initially be formed and trained in a "pure" form, and,
- on the other hand in *complex forms* (strength speed, sprinting strength, etc.), which finally presents the actual practice necessity.

It is absolutely certain that the complex forms require as a basis a high performance level of the "pure" forms, and for a real quantitative increase require a consolidated or specific level of *speed strength* and game-specific *basic endurance*. In addition, naturally, a good level of flexibility.

4.6.2 STRENGTH TRAINING

4.6.2.1 DEFINITION AND METHODICAL HINTS

Strength in sport means the ability of the nerve-muscle system to overcome (concentric work), to work against (eccentric work), or to stop (isometric work) an external resistance by enervation and metabolic processes with muscle contractions.

For practical purposes, the scientifically established strength forms are differentiated as follows:

Maximum strength - the highest possible strength which can consciously be generated against an insurmountable resistance.

Speed strength - the ability of the neuro-muscular system to generate the greatest possible impulse in the time available.

Explosive strength - the maximum strength increase which occurs in a maximally fast muscle contraction.

Reactive strength - the manifestation of strength in the so-called stretch-shortening cycle (consecutive eccentric-concentric functioning of the musculature, e.g. in drop-jumping [plyometric training]).

(Further details cf. Ehlenz et al.; Strength training, BLV Verlag Munich 1998)

Out of all the *different strength forms,* important for the tennis player are maximum strength as a base, and speed strength (also in the form of reactive strength) for kicks, jumping and hitting movements.

In addition to pure speed training we suggest a strength base, which can be trained by two methods, and ultimately leads to a considerable improvement in strength speed.

The so-called *basic method* (beginner's method) represents a complex muscle training programme for all muscles, and should already be used for children aged 8-10. The *speed-oriented maximum strength method* means an increase in tennis-specific maximum strength and can be used from about age 14/16.

Strength Training - Basic Method for Tennis Players
(Methods with light strength effort and medium number of repetitions)

Way of Working:	concentric
Intensity:	medium - load: 40-70%
Movement speed:	fast
Number of exercises:	8-15
Repetitions/exercise:	8-15
Sets/Series:	2-5; rest between series: 1-3 minutes
Periodisation:	2 Training units per week; 3-5 months (in Winter)
Training exercises:	See programmes and exercises below.

Training Effects of the Basic Method

- intra muscular coordination improvement
- muscle cross-section increase
- stabilising of the so-called supporting muscles
- stabilising of the skeleton
- avoidance of, or compensation for, muscular imbalances
- improvement of capillarisation and aerobic-anaerobic metabolism (local muscle endurance)
- decrease in prone to injury.

Training Effects of the Speed-Oriented Maximum Strength Method

- muscle cross-section increase, especially of fast twitch fibres
- improved strength increase
- improved contraction speed
- improvement in aerobic and anaerobic-alactac acid and lactic acid metabolism

We show here with periodisation hints the basic method and speed-oriented maximum strength method, and different exercises for the improvement of all the muscle groups important in tennis.

Speed-oriented Maximum Strength Method
(Method for exhaustive continuous strength effort)

Way of working:	concentric (-eccentric), continuous (fast movement turn-around)
Intensity:	submaximal - load: 40-60%
Movement speed:	as fast as possible
Number of exercises:	8-15
Duration or repetitions per exercise:	up to noticeable loss of speed, about 5-20 seconds; corresponds to 5-15 repetitions
Sets/Series:	3-5; rest between series: 5 minutes or more
Periodisation:	2 training units per week; 3-5 months (in winter/spring)
Training exercises:	See Programmes and exercises that follow.

4.6.2.2 BASIC EXERCISES TO STABILISE THE ABDOMEN AND BACK MUSCLES

Exercise 1

Abdominal muscles 1

The player lies on his back with his legs on a box, hands lie near his bottom. The player slowly lifts the spine from the ground (rolls up), the hands reach for the box. In the final position, the neck and chest vertebrae are not touching the floor. Breathing is calm. The movement speed is slow.

Variations:
- legs are not raised on a box
- at the turning point of the exercise, a stop of 2-4 seconds is carried out

Programme:
8-12 repetitions
3-10 series
1-3 minutes rest

Exercise 2

Abdominal muscles 2

Starting position as in exercise 1, the hands are crossed at the nape of the neck. Roll up slowly with a sideways turn of the spine/axis of the shoulder which should face to the right or left in the final position. This exercise is especially important for the modern tennis technique. Rotation during the stroke is controlled mainly by the oblique abdominal muscles which are worked in this exercise.

Variations and Programme: As above.

Exercise 3

Abdominal muscles 3

The player lies on his back. The legs are bent at right angles and lifted. The hands are on the floor. The player raises and lowers the pelvis by actively tensing the abdominal muscles and pressing the hands on the floor. The knee-hips angle should remain 90°.

Programme: As above

Exercise 4

Back muscles 1

The player lies in prone position, the points of the feet press against the floor. The upper body is straight, with no hollowing of the back. The arms/hands describe movements - lifting - sideways - high bounces - boxing movements to the front - putting the hands together behind the back.

Programme:
10 - 40 seconds
3-5 series
1-3 minute rest

Exercise 5

Back muscles 2

The player on all fours. One arm and the diagonally opposite leg are slowly raised and extended to a horizontal position, without hollowing the back.

For increased difficulty:
The player holds dumbbells (1-3kg), a 2-5 second stop is carried out at the turning point

Programme:
8-20 x left and right
3-8 series
1-3 minute rest

Exercise 6

Back muscles 3

The player lies on his back, the hands press against the floor, the pelvis is slowly raised and lowered again.

Variations:
In the final phase one leg is lifted from the floor and held for about 2-4 seconds.

Programme:
8-15 x (slowly)
3-8 series
1-3 minutes rest

Exercise 7

Stretching exercises for the back muscles

The player lies on his back, the hands wrapped around bent knees. In the initial flexing phase, the head presses against the floor, the hips stretch against the hands for about 2-5 seconds. Now the knees are pulled as near as possible to the upper body, the neck vertebrae are rolled up. This stretch can either be carried out as a simple stretch after each exercise, or as a series of strengthening exercises.

Programme:
15-30 seconds hold,
2-3 x repetitions

4.6.2.3 EXERCISES TO IMPROVE CHEST, SHOULDER AND ARM MUSCLES BY THE BASIC METHOD

Exercise 1 ———————————————— Push-ups

The player lies face down on the floor, the body is straight, the trunk muscles are tensed. The hands are placed beside the shoulders, the finger hints pointing slightly inwards. The player bends and straightens the arms. The upper body does not touch the floor in the starting position.

Variations:
- variation of support width (wide, medium, narrow)
- basic position on the knees (easier)
- basic position with legs on a box (more difficult)

Programme:
8-15 repetitions
2-5 series
1-3 minutes rest

stretching before and after (see exercises 4.6.4.2, no. 8 and 9)

Exercise 2 ———————— Bench press (free weights or machine)

The player lies on his back on a bench, the feet are raised, or the thighs placed vertically. When the weight is pushed up, the player should breathe out. The player bends and straightens the arms quickly.

Variations:
- change the width of the grip (wide, medium, narrow).

Programme:
8-15 repetitions
2-5 series
1-3 minutes rest

stretching before and after, (see exercises 4.6.4.2, no 8 and 9).

Exercise 3

Behind the neck press (free weights or machine)

The player sits in upright position on a small box or similar. Abdominal and back muscles are tensed. Player bends and straightens the arms. The weight is moved perpendicularly upwards from the neck position.

Variations:
* The weight is pushed up alternately from the chest then the neck.

Programme:
8-15 repetitions
2-5 series
1-3 minutes rest

Stretching before and after: (see exercise 4.6.4.2, Nr. 9).

Exercise 4 ——————— Triceps exercises (machine or free weights)

Machine:
The player bends and straightens the arms. The elbows are raised to the level of the upper body.

Free weights:
The player stands or sits, holds the weights with both hands over the head. Player bends and stretches the arms. The elbow movement is always as slight as possible.

Programme:
8-15 repetitions
2-5 series
1-3 minutes rest

stretching before and after
(see exercise 4.6.4.2, Nr. 9)

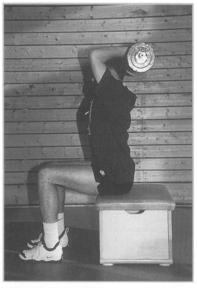

Exercise 5 ——————————— Butterfly (machine or free weights)

Machine:
The player sits in an upright position, back straight. Player brings the bent arms together in front of the breast bone. He should breathe out as he presses them together.

Variations:
* The angle between the trunk and the upper arm is changed

Programme:
8-15 repetitions
2-5 series
1-3 minutes rest

Free weights:
The player lies on his back on a bank/inclined floor. The legs are raised, or the feet are placed on the floor. The dumbbells are brought upwards with bent elbows in circular movements.

Variations:
Inclined bench. According to the degree of incline, different parts of the M. pectoralis major are trained:

Important:
Type of contraction - concentric: fast, eccentric: slow.

Programme:
8-15 repetitions
2-5 series
1-3 minutes rest

stretching before and after (see exercise 4.6.4.2, Nr. 8)

Exercise 6

Reverse flys with dumbbells

The player lies in a prone position on an inclined bench/ flat bench. The arms are brought backwards and upwards with the elbows slightly bent.

Variations:
* the arms are held in the final position for about 2-3 seconds

Programme:
8-15 repetitions
2-5 series
1-3 minutes rest

stretching before and after (see exercises 4.6.4.2, Nr. 6, 8 and 9)

N.B.: For tennis players, the dorsal, the back part of the shoulder muscles is particularly important. Its function is, among others, to pre-tense the working muscles and store energy. It thus makes a fundamental contribution to the action speed of the working muscles.

Exercises with Elastic band (Theraband):

The band is fixed to a stable point. In the starting position it should be slightly taut.

Exercise 7

The player stands facing the fixed point with his arms extended above his head. The arms are moved backwards with a bouncing movement.

The exercise can also be carried out with holding phases.

Exercise 8

Position of feet as in exercise 7. The player brings the arms back bent and straight at shoulder height. Can also be done with holding phases.

Exercise 9

Position of feet as in exercise 7. The player holds the arms perpendicular to the body and moves them backwards. Also possible with holding phases.

Exercise 10

Combination of exercises 7 and 8.

Exercise 11

The player stands with one shoulder towards the fixed point of the band. The arm of the other shoulder is bent at right angles, the upper arm resting against the body. The forearm is moved away from the body. Carry out with left and right arms.

Exercise 12

Starting position as in exercise 11. The arm nearest the fixed point is bent at the elbow, the upper arm lies against the body, the forearm faces the fixed point and is pulled towards the body. Carry out with right and left arms.

Programme:
(For all exercises)

Movement speed: always slow, also with holding phases.

10 to 20 repetitions or until individual exhaustion.

3-8 series
1-2 minutes rest

N.B.: All exercises must be included.

4.6.2.4 EXERCISES TO IMPROVE THE HIP AND LEG MUSCLES BY THE BASIC METHOD

Exercise 1

Squats

The player stands with feet parallel and hip-width apart. The back is straight, the trunk muscles are tensed for stability. For additional loading, a dumb-bell can be carried on the shoulders. The player bends and straightens the legs, concentrically fast and eccentrically slow.

Variations:
Variations in the angle of knee bend, e.g. 1/4 squat, 1/2 squat, full squat.

> *Programme:*
> Intensity/load 40/70%
> 8-15 repetitions
> 2-5 series
> 1-3 minutes rest

Stretching before and after (exercises 4.6.4.2 no 10-13, or 4.6.4.2 no 18).

Exercise 2 ——————————— One-legged squats

The player stands on one leg on a box, bench, etc. By holding on, balance and technical movement execution can be assured. Player bends and straightens the standing leg, the standing foot remains flat on the box. Speed: concentric: fast; eccentric: slow.

Variations:
With additional weight (bar - weighted vest).

> *Programme:*
> 8-15 repetitions
> 2-5 series
> 1-3 minutes rest

Stretching before and after (exercises 4.6.4.2, no 10 to 13, or 4.6.4.2 no 19)

Exercise 3 ——————————— Leg press (machine or partner)

The player lies on his back. Feet are parallel, the trunk muscles are tensed. Player bends and straightens the legs quickly. He should breathe out at the end of the movement.

> *Programme:*
> Load 40-70% - 8-15 repetitions
> 2-5 series
> 1-3 minutes rest

Stretching before and after (exercises 4.6.4.2 no 10-13).

Ankle extension

Exercise 4

The player stands on a small pedestal or step, the heel is lowered below the height of the step, the knees are straightened. The player raises and lowers the body vertically.

Variations:
- both legs, one leg
- with a light additional weight
- in the final position, stand on the balls of the feet and hold for 2-3 seconds
- vary the position of the feet, i.e. toes point inwards or outwards.

Programme:
8-15 repetitions
2-5-series
1-3- minutes one-legged
15-30 repetitions
2-6 series
1-3- minutes two-legged rest

Stretching before and after (exercise 4.6.4.2 no 13)

4.6.2.5 EXERCISES TO IMPROVE THE HIP AND LEG MUSCLES BY THE SPEED-ORIENTED MAXIMUM STRENGTH METHOD

Exercise 1

Two-legged squat (whole leg extension)

The player stands with feet parallel and hip width apart, the back is straight, the trunk muscles are tensed. The player bends and straightens the legs. Effort is continuous (fast movement turn-around) and as fast as possible.

Variations:
Variation in knee angle,
1/3 squat - 1/2 squat

Programme:
Beginners:
Stimulus intensity: 20-30% - 10-15 seconds or
6-10 repetitions
1-3 series
2-5 minutes rest

Advanced:
Stimulus intensity 40-60%, 15-25 seconds or
15-25 repetitions
5 minutes rest or more

Stretching before and after (exercises 4.6.4.2 no 10-13)

Exercise 2 ——— One-legged knee bends (without additional load)

The player stands on one leg on a box, bench, etc. By holding on, balance and technical movement execution are assured. Player bends and straightens the standing leg. Effort is continuous; movement speed as fast as possible.

Programme:
15-25 seconds until noticeable loss of speed
about 15-20 repetitions
3-5 series
3-5 minutes rest

Stretching before and after (exercises 4.6.4.2, no 10-13)

Exercise 3 ——— Leg Press

The player lies on his back. Foot position is parallel, the trunk muscles are tensed. Player straightens and bends the legs continuously and as fast as possible.

Variations:
Different knee angle positions, 1/3 squat, 1/2 squat.

Programme:
Beginners:
Stimulus intensity 20-30%, 10-15 seconds or 6-10 repetitions
1-3 series
3-5 minutes rest

Advanced:
Stimulus intensity 30-60%, 15-25 seconds or
15-25 repetitions
3-5 series
3-5 minutes rest

Stretching before and after (exercises 4.6.4.2, no 10 to 13)

4.6.2.6 EXPLOSIVE STRENGTH EXERCISES TO IMPROVE HIP AND LEG MUSCLES

Exercise 1 ——————————————————

Two-legged extension jumps

The player stands with feet hip-width apart. He bends and straightens the legs with maximum speed, in order to take of maximally high.

Variations:
Different knee angles: 1/3 squats, 1/2 squats, full squat
• carry out jumps for maximal height and maximal length.

Programme:
1/3 squat 8-10 jumps
1/2 squat 5-8 jumps
full squat 2-4 jumps
3-8 series
2-4 minutes rest

Stretching before and after (exercises 4.6.4.2, no 10-13)

Exercise 2 ——————————————————

One-footed extension jumps from fixed knee angle.

The player stands with one leg on a box or chair, etc., with the other leg on the ground. The body is catapulted vertically upwards by a maximally fast extension of the active leg,. The movement starts from the resting position of the active leg, the other leg does not assist. Carry out with the left and right legs.

Variations:
• Change knee angle by changing height of box.
• Add load

Programme:
8-12 repetitions
3-8 series
1-3 minutes rest

Exercise 3

Leg press on Leg press machine

The player lies on his back, feet are hip-width apart. The weight of the body is moved explosively by a maximally fast extension of the legs.

Stretching before and after (exercises 4.6.4.2, no 10-13).

Programme:
8-12 repetitions
3-8 series
1-3 minutes rest

4.6.2.7   REACTIVE STRENGTH EXERCISES TO IMPROVE FOOT, LEG AND HIP MUSCLES

N.B.: for all reactive strength exercises

- maximum short ground contact time

- slight knee bend, heels do not touch the floor

- player must concentrate on the movement

- body tension by contraction of the abdominal and back muscles

- in training, vary all forms of jump (at least 3 types)

- coach encourages verbally

- exercises are mainly suitable for warming up, and are accordingly to be used before every speed training session.

- Stretch before and after (exercises 4.6.4.2, no 10-13)

Exercise 1

Depth jumps

The player stands on a raised surface - 20-40cm - and performs a two-footed depth jump with immediate rebound to another raised surface, with and without the use of arms. Abdominal and back muscles are tensed. Slight knee bend, take-off and landing are on the balls of the feet.

Programme:
8-12 repetitions about 10-15 seconds
rest between jumps.
3-6 series
1-3 minutes rest

Exercise 2

Boundings

The player bounds forwards with one leg, high knee lift of the swing leg, land on the swing leg. The swing leg lands actively and again becomes the jumping leg (reactive). The upper body is upright, abdominal and back muscles are tensed. The arms swing correspondingly.

Programme:
4-10 repetitions/leg
2-6 series
2-3 minutes rest

Exercise 3 — One-footed jumps on right and left leg

The player hops (reactively) vertically upwards and lands again on the take-off leg.

The upper body is upright, the abdominal muscles are tensed. Heels do not touch the ground.

Variations:
- Player hops on the spot
- Player hops forwards
- Hops to a pattern (left>left, right>right, etc.)
- The "inactive" leg is fixed
- The jumping leg is flexed during the hop.

Programme:
6 to maximum 12 repetitions
3-8 series
2-5 minutes rest

Exercise 4 — Sideways bounding (high sideways gallop)

The player performs sideways galloping jumps to the left and right with maximally short ground contact time. Combination of jumping for height and width. The upper body is upright, abdominal and back muscles are tensed.

Programme:
10-20 repetitions
3-8 series
2-4 minutes rest

Stretching before and after (exercises 4.6.4.2, no 12, 14-16)

Exercise 5

Two-footed jumps

The player performs two-footed reactive jumps. The feet are hip-width apart. Abdominal and back muscles are tensed. Very little or no knee bend in the take-off phase.

Variations:
- jump for height or width
- with a ball held between the knees
- jump sideways
- flex the knees in the flight phase

Exercise 6

Jump combinations

The player performs jump combinations of one and two footed jumps, e.g. hops with knees tucked in 2x left and right + 3x two- footed jump + 2x two- footed with flexion of the knee.

Programme:
8-12 repetitions
3-8 series
2-4 minutes rest

movement speed: explosive

4.6.2.8 EXPLOSIVE STRENGTH EXERCISES TO IMPROVE SHOULDER AND ARM MUSCLES

Exercise 1 ——————————————————— Throws

The player kneels on the floor or on a raised surface and holds a medicine ball (1-3kg) in the throwing position. The arms are bent, the upper body is upright.

The player throws the medicine ball forwards with maximum strength effort. Avoid a dynamic back swing. The upper body remains stable. The player aims for high concentration.

Programme:
6-12 repetitions
5-8 series
1-3 minutes rest

Exercise 2 ——————————— Dynamic throw forwards

The player holds the ball with straightened arms in front of the body. The legs are hip-width apart, the upper body is upright. By fast bending (knee angle not greater than 90°) and straightening of the legs and simultaneous maximum fast arm action, the medicine ball is thrown forwards and upwards.

Programme:
6-12 throws
5-8 series
1-2 minutes rest

Two-armed turning throws, forwards, to the left and right. No use of legs.

Exercise 3

The player sits on a box or similar, feet are widely spread for stability - The upper body is upright. The player moves the trunk and arms slowly to the side to prepare the movement swing.

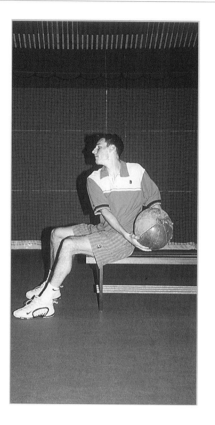

He then turns the trunk fast in the throwing direction and throws the ball with maximum fast throwing action. Perform to the right and left.

Variations:
Throw with one arm with a lighter ball.

Programme:
8-12 repetitions
3-8 series
1-2 minutes rest

Exercise 4

Turning throw using legs, to the right and left.

The player stands in basic position, feet hip-width apart. Player bends both legs, simultaneously turns the trunk and the arms backwards. The player quickly straightens both legs, the upper body is simultaneously turned in the direction of movement and the ball is thrown with a maximum fast arm action.

Variations:
Perform with one arm and a lighter ball.

Programme:
8-12 throws
3-8 series
1-3 minutes rest

Exercise 5

Two-armed turning throw backwards over the right or left shoulder

The player stands with his back to the throwing direction and throws the medicine ball from the starting position, by rapidly straightening the legs and following through with the arms backwards and upwards over the left/right shoulder.

Variations:
Throw without turning backwards right over the head.

Programme:
8-12 repetitions
3-8 series
1-3 minutes rest

Stretching before and after (exercises 4.6.4.2, no 5 and 4.6.4.2 no 10-13) (Also for exercises 1-5)

4.6.2.9 REACTIVE STRENGTH EXERCISES TO IMPROVE SHOULDER AND ARM MUSCLES

Exercise 1 — Short two-armed throws

The player kneels or sits with legs extended and his back leaning against a box. The upper body is upright, the arms in the catching position. Coach/player throws the medicine ball directly into the player's hands. The latter throws the ball back with both hands with a maximum short back swing and arm bend.

Programme:
8-12 repetitions
5-8 series
1-3 minutes rest

Movement speed: explosive

Exercise 2 — Short one-armed throw

The player starts from the same position as exercise 1. The exercise is performed with one arm. Choose a lighter medicine ball. The upper body should remain upright during the throw.

Variations:
Throws should also be carried out with the "wrong" (non favourite) arm.

Programme:
6-10 repetitions
2-6 series
2-4 minutes rest

Exercise 3

Jump push-ups

The player lies prone with bent knees. The hands are shoulder-width apart and turned slightly inwards. By bending and straightening the arms as fast as possible, the upper body is pushed up quickly from the floor. The contact time with the hands on the floor should be as short as possible.

Variations:
Different hand widths: shoulder-width - more than shoulder-width - less than shoulder-width apart.

> *Programme:*
> 6-8 repetitions
> 2-6 series
> 2-4 minutes rest

Exercise 4

Wall Push-up

The player stands close to a wall/sloping surface. Player lets himself fall against this and pushes himself away by straightening his arms and hands as fast as possible. The contact time of the hands against the wall should be as short as possible. Abdominal and back muscles should be tensed. The movement starts from a 1/3 arm bend.

> *Programme:*
> 6-8 repetitions
> 2-6 series
> 2-4 minutes rest

4.6.2.10 EXERCISES TO IMPROVE FOOT AND LEG MUSCLES

General:
A pre-condition for best speed training, and the training of the additional performance-determining conditioning factors, is the optimal function condition of the foot-lower-leg muscles. In all movements, the feet make the first and last contact with the ground, they are exposed to high loads in e.g. braking movements in all jumps. Furthermore, the best function condition of the feet muscles have a not insignificant influence on the body carriage/posture. Many functional irregularities, e.g. of the spine, knees and hips often have their origin in the defective functioning of the foot muscles.

Strength training for foot muscles causes:
• optimal movement performance in speed exercises, jumps, etc.
• a high protection against injury in the ankle area
• a functionally correct body posture.

The exercises can be carried out equally as individual training programmes or as warm-up exercises. They are particularly important in strength training for children and young players. *They should form part of every training session.*

Methodical hints for exercises 4.6.2.10.1-9:
Stimulus duration: exercises 1-9 between 20-60 seconds
Volume: 6-8 exercises
1-3 minutes rest
work tempo: mainly slow stretching before and after
(see chapter 4.6.5.2)
important: - plan the exercises so that as far as possible agonistic and antagonistic muscles are trained consecutively.
- all exercises should also be carried out barefoot.

Toe and Heel lifts

Exercise 1

The player sits on a chair or box. The heel of one foot is raised as is the ball of the other foot. The player now alternately raises and lowers the heels and toes.

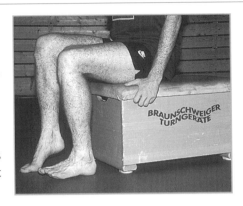

Variation:
The player raises and lowers both heels and balls of the feet at the same time.

Toe movements

Exercise 2

The player sits on the floor. The legs are apart, with the feet touching each other. Open and close only the toes alternately.

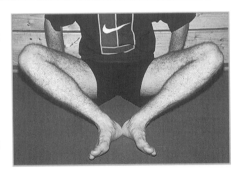

Variation:
The player opens and closes heels and points of the toes.

Changing stand

Exercise 3

The player stands with the body upright in front of a wall/chair and leans on it. By alternately raising and lowering the heels, change between standing on the sole- and tip of toes-position.

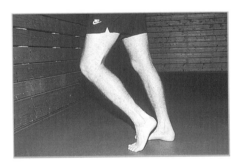

Exercise 4

Ankle straightening

The player stands upright. The legs are crossed. By slowly raising the heels, the body is raised and lowered vertically.

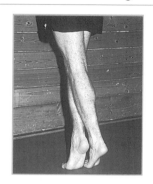

Exercise 5

Medicine Ball stand

The player stands on a medicine ball (3kg). To maintain balance the player can lean on a partner, later he can do the exercise alone. By slight controlled movements of the feet the player can roll the ball in different directions.

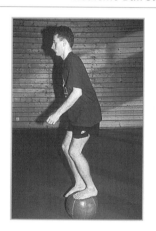

Exercise 6

Sideways Foot Movements

The player stands in the starting position. The feet are hip-width apart, the toes/heels turned towards each other. By moving the feet sideways by simultaneously turning either the heels or toes, the player moves sideways. The exercise is carried out both to the right and left.

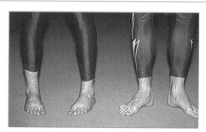

Exercise 7 — Pole stand

The player stands upright on a pole. By shifting balance, the pole can slowly be rolled along.

Exercise 8 — Foot tilting

The player stands in the starting position, the feet slightly opened. By tilting the feet, carry out a continuous change between standing on the soles and on the outside edge of the feet.

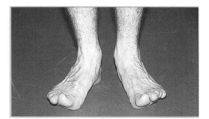

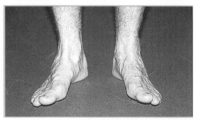

Exercise 9 — Foot lifting

The player stands or sits upright. One foot rests on the other. The player tries, against the resistance of the upper foot, to lift it with the lower one.

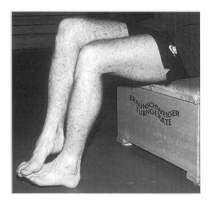

Programme:
For static work, about 5-8 times 8 to 10 seconds holding, then dynamic work 20 to 60 seconds.

Exercise 10 —————————————— Ankle bending

The player squats very low. He raises his body by flexing the feet. An upright body position is important, the knees should not be straightened. The exercise can also be carried out one-footed, alternately left and right. *Movement speed:* mainly slow.

Programme:

Two-footed:	one-footed:
10-20 repetitions	6-10 repetitions
3-5 series	3-5 series
1-3 minutes rest	1-3 minutes rest

Stretching before and after (exercise 4.6.4.2, no 13)

Exercise 11 —————————————— Sideways Ankle Movement

The player stands in starting position, feet are parallel and hip-width apart. Then carry out a sideways movement by alternately putting weight on the heels and balls of the feet and simultaneously turning in the direction of movement. Perform to the right and left. The body is tensed, no bending of the hips.

Programme:
8-12 x to left and right = 1 series
4-8 series
1-2 minutes rest

Stretching before and after (exercise 4.6.4.2 no 13)

Exercise 12

Ankle Jumps

The player stands in starting position. Heels or toes are turned towards each other. The player makes small jumping movements from the ankle, without bending the knee. Short ground-contact time, body tension.

Programme:
15-30 jumps
2-6 series
1-3 minutes rest

Stretching before and after (exercise 4.6.4.2, no 13)

Variations:
• only heels or only toes turn towards each other.
• in every jump, heels and toes turn alternately towards each other
• arms above the head, holding a light weight (medicine ball)

Exercise 13

Rope Skipping

Two-legged rope skipping with short ground-contact time and high frequency. One jump for every turn of the rope.

Variations:
• one foot is placed in front of the other and alternated on every rope swing
• the feet are placed alternately together and then about shoulder-width apart
• the feet are placed one after the other on a circle line while jumping.

Programme:
20-60 seconds
5-15 series
1-3 minutes rest

Stretching afterwards (exercise 4.6.4.2, no. 13)

Exercise 14

Toe gripping

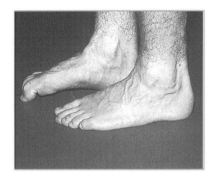

The player stands upright in the basic position. By activating the foot muscules, "toe-gripping", he tries to move the body forwards.

Programme:
10-30 seconds
3-8 series
1-3 minutes rest

Exercise 15

Two-legged ankle work

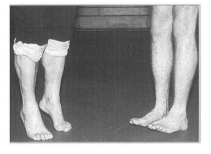

The player stands upright and keeps his body tense. He alternately transfers his body weight between his heels and his feet.

Programme:
30-60 seconds
3-5 series
1-3 minutes rest

4.6.3 ENDURANCE TRAINING

4.6.3.1 DEFINITION AND METHODICAL HINTS

Endurance means generally the ability to resist a tiring load mentally and physically for a long time, and/or to recover quickly from physical and mental demands. In sport we differentiate between basic endurance and special endurance. Only the first type is particularly important for tennis players, and then with the following functions:

- *increasing the ability to stand hard work during extensive loading work rate* in training and competition (e.g. in technique and match training, and in long matches and/or long tournaments). Endurance has a fundamental influence on the development and realisation of other abilities and skills;
- *acceleration of recovery* after training and tournaments (regeneration);
- endurance also accomplishes the *task of maintaining* health and fitness.

Extensive (Continuous) Endurance Method (for endurance "beginners")

Movement forms:	Running/jogging, walking, cycling, cross-country skiing, ergometer - riding and rowing.
Load intensity:	In the area of 60-75% of heart circulation performance, that means a pulse rate of about 135-165 (according to age and performance level), or about 2-2.5 mmol lacate *Pulse rate-rule of thumb* • for beginners: 160 minus age • for advanced: 170 minus 1/2 age +/- 10 per minute
Load duration for equal speed or effort:	Minimum 20 minutes, maximum 60 minutes (including slow warm-up and warm-down)
Training frequency per week:	• to improve basic endurance in the winter months: 3-5 x or 2-4 hours in total per week. • As a recovery session, and to maintain general aerobic capacity during competition phase: 2 x or 60-90 minutes in total per week.

From the canon of endurance methods, we consider that for the *improvement of basic endurance the extensive* (for endurance "beginners"), and the *variable* (for advanced) *continous methods* are particularly suitable for tennis players. The training advantage of these methods, lies mainly in the relatively long duration of loading, in which the intensity-dependent physiological process runs quite constantly. There is an economy of the organ functions on the one hand, and on the other a improvement of the organ system. The player also gets mentally used to the monotony of training.

The necessity for an improvement in basic endurance for *young tennis players* occurs at around 12 years. Although biologically suitable conditions for endurance improvement already exist at around ages 6/8 , we consider it wise to save "profitable" training until later.

Training effects of the extensive continous method
- economising of the heart circulation work
- improvement of the peripheral blood supply
- expansion of the aerobic metabolism and improved fat-burning
- development of Vagotonie (= predominance of parasympathetic)

Training effects of the variable endurance method
- adaptations in the heart circulation system and the skeleton muscles
- improved transition between the purely aerobic (fatty acid/glycogen burning) energy preparation
- improved lactate compensation and elimination in the extensive loading phases.

Variable Endurance method (for endurance-advanced)
All components of the extensive endurance method are also present here; there is just a difference in the variation of the movement speed: between slow and fast, and therefore naturally in the loading intensity:
Pulse rate between 130 and 180 or lactate between 2 and 6 mmol

4.6.3.2 TRAINING PROGRAMMES

Table 6:

Sample programme to improve basic endurance by running* according to the extensive endurance method for those with no endurance training background

week	1-2	3-4	5-6	7-8	9-10	11-12	13-14	15-16	cont.
run (min)	20	25	30	30	35	40	35	30	30
pulse rate (min) age 14-17 age 18-25	150 130-140	150 140	160 140-150	160 150	170 150-160	170 150-160	170 160	170 160	160 150
training units/ week	3	3	3	4	4	4-5	4-5	4	2-3

* The programme can also be carried out with other endurance exercises, such as cycling, ergometer, etc. The important factor is the maintenance of the pulse-rate.

Table 7:

Sample programme to improve basic endurance by running according to the variable endurance method for those with endurance experience.

week	1-2	3-4	5-6	7-8	9-10	11-12	13-14	15-16
run (min)	20	30	30 40	20 30	3x10 5 mins rest*			
pulse rate/min** age 18-25	130-150	130-160	130-180	150-180	150-180	150-180	140-170	130-130
training units	3	3	3	4	3-4	3-4	3	2-3

* in the rests: 1 minute walking, 3 minutes short starts, 1 minute walking.
** 14-17 year-olds, about 10-15 beats higher.

4.6.4 FLEXIBILITY TRAINING

4.6.4.1 DEFINITION AND METHODICAL HINTS

Flexibility (also called mobility) is a basic pre-condition for technically successful and fast movement execution. Parallel with the development of all conditioning and coordination technical abilities and skills an improvement, or maintenance, of flexibility must always be aimed for.

Flexibility is the ability to carry out conscious movements within a greater range in certain joints. Flexibility is formed from the components of *agility* (= concerns passive movement apparatus) and *stretchability* (= concerns active movement apparatus).

Training Methods for Simple Stretching (passive-static stretching)
(1) Stretch the relevant muscle groups slowly and carefully; hold about 8-10 seconds - then the muscles will be noticeably "softer";
(2) then stretch a little further and hold for 10-20 seconds
The stretches do not have to be timed to the exact second, the player should be able to feel the required tensing and relaxing of each muscle.
Repetitions: 2-5 per muscle group

Training Methods for dynamic-elastic (ballistic) stretching (swinging)
Exercise execution:
Swinging-rocking movement up to respective movement swing-limit.
3-4 exercises per area of the body - about 15 to 20 in total, with 10-15 repetitions each.
All exercises should be increased gradually; be careful of over-stretching!
Loosen-up the muscles after each repetition.

- *Poor flexibility* can lead to the following consequences: an increased risk of injury; an uneconomical execution of speed and strength activities and movement techniques; a delayed learning of new movements.

- In tennis one can observe children with a *pronounced muscular imbalance*, that means e.g. a muscular imbalance between well-trained leg muscles and substantially weaker trunk and shoulder muscles. Later on, muscle shortening and weakness in certain parts of the body can be seen.
- By targeted stretching of inflexible muscles, and targeted strengthening of weak muscles, these negative phenomena can be counteracted.
- Finally, a top performance development in tennis without the relevant stretching ability is impossible. Referring to the *different methods* to improve or maintain flexibility, we recommend to tennis players the two methods explained on the previous page.

Practical Applications of Stretching

1 Stretch before every training session and tournament match.
2. Stretch between separate speed, strength or technique series (about 2x10 seconds of light stretching).
3. Stretch after a training unit or tournament match. This shortens the subsequent recovery process.

4.6.4.2 EXERCISES TO IMPROVE FLEXIBILITY

Back Stretching exercises

Exercise 1

The player lies on his/her back, the thighs are vertical. The thighs are pulled downwards towards the trunk, the chin is slightly pulled in to the chest. The stretching position is held. Gentle breathing.

Exercise 2

The player is on all fours. By moving the spine upwards and downwards alternate slowly between the "cat hump" and "hollow back".

Exercise 3

The player sits on a box, bends the upper body forwards gently. The stretch can be increased by pulling with the hands.

Stretching Exercises for Chest-Neck-Nape of the Neck

Exercise 4

The player sits on a chair with the head to one side, the opposite shoulder is actively pulled down.

Variations:
By varying the position of the chin, different muscles can be strongly stretched.

Exercise 5

The player sits on a box. The arms are placed backwards and upwards on the wall. The upper body, with a straight back, is bent forwards (external rotation of the shoulder joints).

Variations:

- Vary the height and width of the arms.
- the exercise is carried out with the right and left arms.

Exercise 6

The player stands upright, with trunk and back muscles tensed. One arm is extended in front of the body so that the little finger is pointing upwards. The extended arm is pulled towards the body without turning the shoulders (external rotation of the shoulder joint).

Variations:

- Stretch the arms so that the thumb points upwards (internal rotation).
- the exercise is carried out with the left and right arms.

Exercise 7

The player sits upright on a chair or box. The head is bent forwards, and can be assisted by careful pulling with the hands. The upper body remains upright.

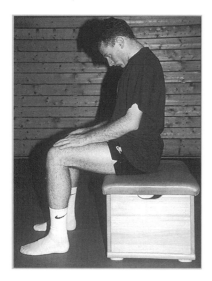

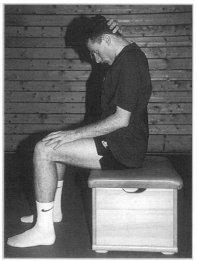

Exercise 8

The player stands upright. The position of the upper arm is horizontal, the forearm and the edge of the little finger are resting against a wall. The trunk is turned away forwards by the arm.

Variations:
- The height of the forearm can be varied.
- The exercise is carried out with the right and left arm.

Stretching Exercises for Hips and Legs

Exercise 9

The player sits or stands with the body upright. One upper arm is vertical, the other horizontal. The hand points towards the opposite shoulder. The opposite hand pulls the bent arm behind the head to the opposite shoulder. Carry out to the right and left.

Exercise 10

The player stands in front of a chair or box or similar. The heel of one leg is placed on the chair, the hints of the toes are turned inwards. The back is tilted forwards and the hips bent.

Exercise 11

The player makes a big stride forwards, the upper body leans on the thigh, the hands support on the floor. The hips are pressed towards the floor. Carry out with right and left legs.

Variations:
• The upper body is upright and the knee of the back leg touches the floor.

Exercise 12

The player lies on his/her side, the forearm supports the upper body. The top leg is bent backwards. The lower leg is now pulled towards the bottom. Carry out with right and left leg.

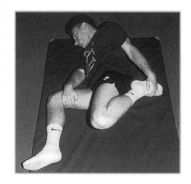

Exercise 13

The player stands in front of a wall and supports him/herself against it. The rear leg is straightened, the front leg bent. The heel of the rear leg is touching the floor. The hips are now pushed towards the wall. Carry out with right and left legs. This stretches the two insertions of the calf muscle.

Variations:

* Bending of the back leg at the knee, to stretch the lower part of the calf muscle (stretching of the soleus muscle).

Stretching of the Adductors

Exercise 14

The player sits in an upright position, with legs bent, the knees pointing upwards, the upper body is upright. The feet are brought in close to the hips. The knees lie on the floor or push downwards towards the floor.

Exercise 15

The player stands with his legs astride, the legs are more than hip-width apart. The body weight is over one leg, until the knee is half-bent. The other leg remains straight. Carry out with right and left legs.

Exercises for Abductor Muscles

Exercise 16

The player stands upright with legs crossed. The body weight is placed to one side. The direction of the movement is to the right if the left leg is in front, and vice versa.

Exercises for the "Dynamic-ballistic stretching" Training Method

Exercise 17

The arms are swung backwards alternately in three stages up to the limit of movement, the upper body remains upright.

Programme:
15-20 repetitions per level.

Exercises for Arms and Shoulders

Exercise 18

The player stands upright. One hand can be used for support to keep balance. The upper body remains upright.

* Player swings one leg with deliberate emphasis forwards and upwards. Carry out with right and left leg.
* Player swings one leg with deliberate emphasis backwards and upwards. Carry out with right and left leg.

Programme:
15-20 repetitions per level.

Exercise 19

The player stands upright. He can support himself to keep balance.

* Player swings one leg with deliberate emphasis sideways and upwards. Carry out with right and left legs.

Programme:
15-20 repetitions per level.

Exercise for Abdominal Muscles

Exercise 20

The player lies in a prone position, the hands placed on the floor at shoulder level. By straightening the arms, the upper body is pushed slowly upwards and backwards. The head should be in line with the body.

Variations:
At the end of the movement, hold for 3-5 seconds.

Programme:
3-4 repetitions = 1 series
2-3 series
work slowly

5 TRAINING PROGRAMMES FOR SHORT AND MEDIUM-TERM PLANNING

5.1 TRAINING PROGRAMMES FOR TRAINING UNITS

As already mentioned, speed training must take place from a state of complete recovery, be carried out at maximum intensity and the technical quality must be high.

Certain *guidelines for the pattern of speed training within a training unit can* already be deduced from these conditions. (cf also 4.1 General Methodical Instructions):

1. Speed training must come at the beginning, not the end, of a training session. *Technique and tactical training must follow.*

2. If one wants to dedicate a whole training unit exclusively to speed training as *the main unit of the day,* then one should allow a long time, because sufficient rest to enable complete recovery must always be programmed between individual exercises. About 1 1/2 hours will suffice.

3. The combination of *separate training forms* within a training unit must be carefully planned according to the following guidelines:

a) Different speed types should always be included in a training unit.

b) The exercise forms should be combined in such a way that both areas - the area of special training forms, as well as the area of tennis-specific training forms - alternate with each other, in order to ensure direct integration into the tennis technique.

c) In planning, care should be taken that the individual areas of emphasis, such as arms, upper body and legs are always alternated within a training unit, so as to prevent overloading or neglect of one area.

d) In team or group training, individual differences and requirements (fitness level, condition, age, sex, etc.) must be considered. That means that the number of repetitions, series, length of rest, additional loading, level of difficulty and quality of performance must be suited to each player.

4. Tennis is able to offer other training alternatives though, which can, at least partially, compensate for the disadvantages or difficulties of a single long speed unit.

For example, speed training can be included in practically every training programme. It is well-known that not more than 30 minutes should be spent on the single technique or tactical part of a training session, apart from specific exceptions. Afterwards, rests of 3-5 minutes should be programmed, before continuing with the next part of the training unit (Schönborn 1994).

5. There is automatically the possibility, right after the general and specific warm-up, to begin with one of the above mentioned speed drills. In addition, after the first rest, another speed drill can be introduced, and if the rest of the training is not too demanding, after the second, somewhat longer rest, begin the next part with a third speed drill. These drills do not take much time, and two or three per day can be done, which in a 5-day micro-cycle means 10-15 speed drills. That is 40-60 drills per month. Care should be taken that the individual drills are carried out in their entirety and at high intensity, as set out in the descriptions above.

6. In addition, further tennis-specific drills can be integrated into technique training and can later be incorporated in the form of complex training (Schönborn 1995). Of course, this does not mean that separate speed training is unnecessary, it just needs to be done less often and for less time, saving a lot of time.

5.1.1. SUGGESTIONS FOR THE PLANNING OF TRAINING UNITS

In the model, a new concept is presented, which simplifies the process of planning a training unit. This model is valid for all abilities and ages, independently of whether it is a training unit in the gym or on the tennis court, or both.

Explanations
• A compact speed training unit should be scheduled twice per week. In an emergency only one unit per week can take place; in which case, daily speed drills must be carried out in the context of technique or tactical training (see main section).

Warm-up phase
• The warm-up phase should begin with a three to five minute varied run, forwards, sideways, hopping, side-stepping, skipping, bounding, with the inclusion of balls, small games, etc,
• the warm-up phase should always include strengthening exercises,
• the stretching programme should always precede the strengthening exercises,
• the warm-up phase should be carried out calmly, unhurriedly and without time pressure,
• it should last at least 15 minutes, preferably 20.

Main section
• Individual blocks can be left out of the planning, but the order must always be maintained.
• Basically, individual areas (arms, legs, body) must be alternated in the programme, so that e.g. all three blocks do not concentrate on the legs. This is not just because of a possible over-loading of the selected area, but also for the sake of variety. Of course, exceptions are possible, especially, for example, where the training of frequency speed prepares the training of time-programmes.

- The time data are intended as suggestions, based on years of experience. In special cases, or with large groups, or for particular objectives, these ranges can be extended.
- Where there are time problems that necessitate the reduction of the length of a unit to e.g. one hour, the main section must be shortened at one block.
- Care should be taken that the tennis-specific exercises with ball and racquet are regularly alternated with the specific exercises, and above all that all exercise forms are combined with technique training and flow into this.
- To this end it is recommended that speed training, in addition to the compact speed units, is included daily in each training unit, as described in 5.1.

Endpart
- The endpart also serves as an introduction to the recovery phase:
- By means of exercise forms in the aerobic area, e.g. slow running, cycling (approx. 2mmol/1, 120 bpm), ball games for motivation, the blood circulation is stimulated which thereby accelerates the elimination of burnt substrates.
- Stretching loosens and de-cramps muscles which were called on in the main phase.
- Massage and sauna likewise activate the blood circulation and also help psychological recovery.

Table 8:
Suggestion for the structure of training units in tennis speed training

Warm-up *20 minutes*	• general movement forms with or without ball • running, hopping, sidesteps, rope jumps etc in different directions • stretching of the relevant parts of the body • strength training forms to sensitise the working and supporting muscles • ball games (eg football-tennis, etc)
Main Section *80 min*	Combination of the contents of blocks 1-3 (only one) or two exercises from each of the following blocks should be selected and used)
Block 1 *25 minutes*	4.2 Training of time-programmes 4.3 Training of reaction and action speed
Block 2 *25 minutes*	4.4 Training of frequency speed
Block 3 *30 minutes*	4.5 Combined training of action, frequency, and strength speed as well as coordination abilities 4.6 Training of additional performance-determining conditioning abilities
Endpart *15 minutes*	• ball games according to choice (for motivation) • strength training (e.g. abdominals and back) • extensive slow running or cycling • stretching (long hold method) • sauna, massage

TRAINING PROGRAMME
FOR MICROCYCLES
5.2

A one-week programme is not only dependent on age, sex, state of fitness, etc., but also on the training period.

Different contents, loads, volumes, intensities etc. corresponding to the goals of the individual periods must be considered. So, for example, in the first part of the preparation period, the emphasis lies on specific training and on the quality of the performance in the individual areas 4.2, 4.3, 4.4 as well as on the training supplementing performance-determining conditioning abilities (4.6).

In the second part of this period, in which maximum intensity must be aimed for, tennis-specific speed should predominate (4.3, 4.4 and 4.5). In addition, the integration of the individual speed components into the tennis technique, and above all into situation-solving must be totally guaranteed.

In the competition period the acquired speed level must at least be maintained, by above all selective highly intensive short loads (no fatigue), and choosing training forms which always correspond to a match-type situation. The tennis-specific situational transfer must be further increased, which indeed happens directly in a match, but in training should not be neglected.

In short and medium-term planning, care must be taken that the exercise forms suggested in this book are actually used, that they are all alternated, but included regularly, to avoid reaching a possible barrier.

BIBLIOGRAPHY

Adams; G.R. et al.: Skeletal muscle mysin heavy chain composition and resistance training. In: J. Appl. Physiol. 74 (1993) 2, 911-915.

Asmus, S.A.: Physische und motorische Entwicklung im Kindes- und Jugendalter. Kassel 1991 und 1994.

Bauersfeld, M./Voss, G.: Neue Wege im Schnelligkeitstraining. Münster 1992.

Baur, J. et al. (Hrsg.): Motorische Entwicklung. Schondorf 1994.

Born, H.-P. et al. (Hrsg.): Schnelligkeit im Tennis. (6. Symoisium des Ausschusses für Sportwissenschaft des DTB. Göttingen 1996.) Hamburg 1997.

Charitonova, L. G.: Theoretische und experimentelle Begründung von Adaptationstypen im Sport. In: Leistungssport 23 (1993) 2/3, 40-43.

Ehlenz, H. et. al.: Krafttraininng. München 1998.

Grosser, M.: Schnelligkeitstraining. München 1991.

Grosser, M./Starischka, St.: Konditionstests. München 1986.

Grosser, M./Starischka, St.: Das neue Konditionstraining. München 1998.

Hoppeler, H.: Strukturelle und funktionelle Grundlagen der Schnelligkeit. Vortrag 'Trainerseminar Schnelligkeit', 3.-5. April 1992, Stuttgart.

Lehmann, F.: Schnelligkeitstraining im Sprint. In: Leichtathletiktraining (1993), Sep./Okt.

Martin, D. et al.: Handbuch Trainingslehre. Schorndorf 1991.

Schmalz, Th./Türk-Noack, K.: Geschwindigkeitsmessung mit Laserdiodentechnik. In: Leistungssport 23 (1993) 6.

Schönborn, R.: Vortrag beim ITF Worldwide Workshop 1994.

Schönborn. R.: Vortrag beim DTB/VDT Bundeskongress 1995.

Staron, R.A. et al.: Strength und Skeletal muscle adaptions heavy-resistance-trained woman after detraining und retraining. In: J. Appl. Physiol. 70 (1991) 2, 631-640.

Tidow, G.: Schnelligkeitstraining unter besonderer Berücksichtigung der Kraftfähigkeit. In: Born, H.-P. et al. (Hrsg.): Schnelligkeit im Tennis. Hamburg 1997, 45-67.

Tidow, G./Wiemann, K.: Zur Interpretation und Veränderbarkeit von Kraft-Zeit-Kurven bei explosiv-balltstischen Krafteinsätzen. In: Dt. Zs. f. Sportmedizin (1993). Hefte 3, 4

Voss, G./Werthner, R.: Leistungs- und Talentdiagnostik. In: Leistungssport 24 (1994) 4.

Weigelt, St.: Zum trainingswissenschaftlichen Modell der Schnelligkeit. In: *Nicolaus, J./Zimmermann, K. W. (Red.):* Sportwissenschaft interdisziplinär. Kassel 1995, 149-160.

Weineck, J.: Sportbiologie. Erlangen 1994.

Manfred Grosser
A graduate in Psychology, he is professor of movement and training theory at the University of Munich, and secondary official lecturer at the Cologne Coaching Academy and in the coaching education of several federations. He is a former high-level sportsman (100m: 10.5 seconds; upper league tennis player) and has many years experience of coaching elite athletes.

Heinz Kraft
Qualified sport coach and B-coach, he is conditioning coach for the German Tennis Federation (DTB). He is responsible for the conditioning training of pool players of the DTB in the national training centre in Hannover and is active in the initial and further training of coaches in the DTB and VDT. In addition, he teaches tennis at grass roots level and advises clubs on the organisation and implementation of suitable training for young players.

Richard Schönborn
A-coach, for 26 years was Head coach of the German Tennis Federation (DTB) and Davis Cup and Federation Cup coach. In his playing days, he was National Champion, Tournament winner of 31 National and International tournaments and member of the Czechoslovak Davis Cup Team. Today, he works as lecturer in the Cologne Coaching Academy and for the International Tennis Federation world-wide in the coaches and players education.